THE SUMMER PARTY

His largest and most ambitious play to date, 1
Poliakoff's obsession with youth culture and a
portrayal. The central character is a high-flyin͙   ͙͙ͺ͙ͺͺͺaͻͻie, Kramer, who
ends up being the star of the show he has come to patrol. Like all Poliakoff's major
portrayals, Kramer's life and philosophy is physically contained on the stage by
both an area designed for his operation and a symbolic car that represents
authority and his bed for the night. The rest is a tree and a green sward, where a
distraught sponsor, his photographer wife, a detained typist, and two well-
contrasted policemen, fill in the picture.'

Michael Coveney, *Financial Times*

'It is a typical open-air rock concert. The stars, having made impossible demands
before signing their contract, have failed to turn up. A singer refuses to go back on
stage after his 30-minute act even to stop the angry audience rioting. A young
performer breaks down in mid-performance. The laser light show doesn't work.
There are 37 toilets for thousands of people and a boy is stabbed because he stood
in front of another fan. Its rich young promoter, who sees himself as the Rock
Age's Great Gatsby and aims to get richer, describes it all as "a celebration".
Stephen Poliakoff's ironically titled play springs a few surprises by keeping these
disorderly events on the periphery and concentrating instead on the collusion
between the police and those who, in the popular imagination, are rebels: rock
singers and impresarios. . . . Poliakoff brilliantly emphasises their infantile
behaviour by bringing on an actual child, a fraudulent punk psychic, whose
monstrous behaviour, full of foot-stamping tantrums, is indistinguishable from
that of his elders. . . . Marvellous in suggesting our febrile times and full of sour
insights into the moral squalor of rock.'

John Walker, *Now!*

'. . . a scarey, profound and prophetic picture of pop in the 1980s as it hasn't quite
happened yet'.

Daily Mail

'a shocker of a new play – a play for tomorrow as much as today . . . There is
conflict a-plenty: fringe versus establishment, fuzz versus ravers, pop versus punk,
age versus youth, and the threat of mass hysteria turning into mob violence. The
mood of menace is marvellously sustained . . .'

Daily Express

THE
SUMMER PARTY

STEPHEN POLIAKOFF

A Methuen New Theatrescript
Eyre Methuen · London

First published in 1980 by Eyre Methuen Ltd, 11 New Fetter Lane,
London EC4P 4EE
Copyright © 1980 by Stephen Poliakoff
Printed in Great Britain by Expression Printers Ltd, London N1

ISBN 0 413 47600 6

The Summer Party was first performed at the Sheffield Crucible Theatre on 12 March 1980, with the following cast:

KRAMER	Brian Cox
CAROLINE	Patti Love
LOUISE	Hayley Mills
NIGEL	Alan Rickman
KEN	Peter Schofield
JOHN	Roger Lloyd-Pack
STEPHEN	Mark Drewry
DAVID	Dexter Fletcher
KID	Patrick Murray

Directed by Peter James
Designed by Roger Glossop

The time is the present.

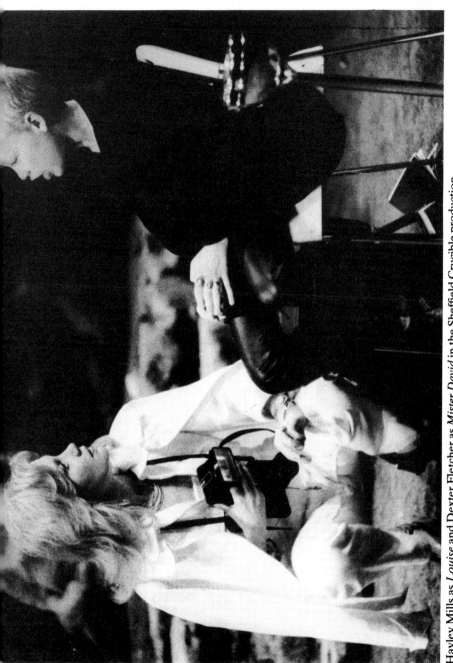

Hayley Mills as *Louise* and Dexter Fletcher as *Mister David* in the Sheffield Crucible production.
Photo: Viewfinder Associates

Roger Lloyd-Pack as *John* and, in background, Brian Cox (*Kramer*) and Mark Drewry (*Stephen*). Photo Viewfinder Associates

Act One

As the house lights dim, we hear the noise of
a crowd waiting, the sound of voices and
paper rustling round the audience, then
SIMON breaks through, loud and direct
as if through a Public Address system.

SIMON'S VOICE (*through Public*
Address): Now we have just a bit of a
break before our next act comes up here.
So there's a little time for you to stretch
your legs, shake hands with your
neighbour if you haven't already done so,
and if you want to that is; and take a look
around.

Just to remind you, food, First Aid and
toilet facilities are provided in ample
supply by the East Gate . . . , that's the
East Gate. And a further reminder if you
lose anything, then Lost Property is by
the South Gate. But please try to keep
your litter with you, just wrap it up into a
very small ball and put it back in your bags
where it came from. Remember this field
has got to be used again. Thank you
friends, see you in a bit.

Music comes up and as the curtain goes up
the music fades into the distance as if we
are hearing it from several hundred yards
away. During the first scene it fades out.
We are outside the perimeter of the festival.
Bright summer evening light. The
cyclorama is a pale evening blue.
Down the whole length of stage left is a
narrow marquee or canvas awning,
covering a very long trestle table, the sort
seen at enormous receptions. We cannot at
this stage see what is on the table because it
is covered in thick muslin to protect it from
the insects.
On the other side of the stage is a large
police car, a black BMW spotless and
shining, parked upstage.
The stage is covered in grass, which has the
yellowish, tawny look of midsummer. Arc
lights and possibly a string of coloured
lights on the marquee stare down on the
action. These lights are not switched on
yet. A few white chairs are grouped by the
table. Also stage left and separate from the
main table, large metal coffee urn and tea
urns.
LOUISE is standing stage right. She is
thirty-four. Wearing a long dress, she has
red hair. She is smoking a cigarette, sharp
intelligent eyes. An expensive camera is
slung over her arm.

KEN, a Police Superintendant of about
fifty, stands stage left. He is in uniform. A
big heavily-built man.
CAROLINE is sitting on the ground just
by him. She is in her mid-twenties, with
black curly hair. She is dressed in a denim
skirt and a summer blouse.
Mid-stage is NIGEL. He is thirty-six years
old. He is dressed in a beautifully cut white
suit. He has dark hair, a sharp but very
charming smile and manner. His voice has
a natural effortless upper-middle-class
authority. He is holding a compact,
gleaming walkie-talkie radio. He flicks it
on.

NIGEL (*into the walkie-talkie*): Simon . . .
yes, we've arrived up here . . . he was two
minutes short on his last number, yes,
rather cut price. (*Charming smile.*) But I
think we'll let him get away with it.

That tiny fudge on the speaker has gone.
Yes, there was just a very slight slurring
(*He smiles into the machine.*) Or maybe
that's how you speak normally. Yes,
they're not bad are they, de luxe from
Philips. Tony Bennett used them in
Houston last month. (*He smiles.*) It says
so on the boxes.

Yes just a little ironing out required . . .
but they seem to have made a job of it, yes
there's no overloading.

Now; you are keeping the exact position
of this area here quiet aren't you. Only
those strictly specified . . . I'm sure you
are. (*He smiles.*) Just so long as there are
no vast notices going up pointing in this
direction – or maps being handed out to
the audience (*sharp*). Good.

LOUISE (*broad smile*): I'm sure they
wouldn't tell, not even under torture.

NIGEL (*glancing round the location as he*
holds the radio): No, no, it seems fine.
We're just having another look at it now.
Yes, we'll get an excellent view of the
lazer show up here.
There's a strong rather pleasant smell of
something. (*Smiles.*) No, some flower.

LOUISE: Honeysuckle.

NIGEL: It's honeysuckle, I've been reliably
informed. (*He glances down.*) It almost
looks as if the grass has been specially
mown for them all (*Smiles.*). Slightly
overdoing it I feel . . . A marked absence
of insects – we've obviously managed to

pay them off; or assasinated the entire population.

(*Sharp.*) Do I want to speak to who? Absolutely no member of the media yet – *no* . . . which one is it? . . . Him, the one with a permanent nose bleed. (*Charming smile.*) No I don't know why, maybe he just keeps bumping into things. Give him half a glass of cider and put him behind a bush. How's the GATE going? . . . Good. All lines of communication seem to be functioning. (*He flicks off the walkie-talkie with a sharp movement.*)

(*He glances at KEN, sharp smile.*) I can see how people can get addicted to using those things – start screaming when they're parted from them. (*At* KEN:) You must find that?

KEN (*uneasy*): I can't say I have.

NIGEL (*glancing down at the walkie-talkie – grins at* KEN): It's a new model with an improved gossamer thin ariel.

LOUISE (*smiling*): I think it looks terrific here, very inviting.

NIGEL (*surveying it*): Not bad. The shape's right. The position's reasonable. (*He glances straight at* KEN – *polite smile.*) There's just one thing I'd like to know . . . that girl there.

KEN: Don't worry about her. She's being held for questioning.

NIGEL (*smiles*). For questioning? Been misbehaving? (*Glancing at* CAROLINE.) That's rather quick work isn't it. (*Charming smile.*) I will pry no further.

KEN: This has to be a transit point I'm afraid – vehicles can't get down any further. And they can turn round here.

NIGEL (*smiles straight at* KEN): That's exactly why it was selected.

KEN: When a car's available we'll be moving her.

NIGEL: I'm sure you will. (*He moves, glancing over the spot.*) It's rather harder to gain entry to this spot here, than to the Royal Enclosure at Ascot. (*Charming smile.*) – at least that was the intention. We've been very selective . . .

(*to* KEN): It's for the top half of the bill playing here tonight, which we're now

getting to. (*He smiles.*) an exclusive place . . . the ground is mined in every direction, and there're mantraps in the long grass, all the way round. (*Glances at* KEN, *polite smile.*) That's not to be taken literally.

Pause. KEN shuffles.

KEN: If I may say so, the site for the whole occasion is very well chosen.

NIGEL (*glances up*). Thank you. Yes, access is good, the station reasonably close, special late night train scheduled, if British Rail is to be trusted. (*He moves.*) I sent people off to sit in practically every field in southern England (*Charming smile.*) It took longer than I expected – they all turned out to be terrified of cattle. I had to find a place where there were no low flying aircraft or nudist colonies.

LOUISE (*smoking*): Not as simple as it may seem.

NIGEL: Precisely.

LOUISE: They stumbled on quite a few, didn't they?

NIGEL (*to* LOUISE, *quietly, indicating camera*): Have you actually taken any yet?

LOUISE: No (*Smiles.*) Not one shot. It's a virgin piece of film. The light's just getting right now. I've got so much film here.

NIGEL (*smiles at her*). Is it colour or black and white?

LOUISE: I should think they'll come out sort of sepia – as they normally do.

NIGEL: That's nonsense – they'll be splashing all over those shiny unreadable magazines, which always come out months after the event. Soft focus stills.

LOUISE (*smiling*). Or out of focus.

NIGEL (*much quieter*): You look rather striking tonight.

LOUISE (*smiles*). Do I?

NIGEL Yes. (*Back on the walkie-talkie.*) Yes, Simon? Fine. Remember, we have done a deal to sell those afterwards. I'm right in thinking there have been no forged tickets yet . . . so having those complicated graphics actually worked. Yes, they are nice – I designed them myself. (*Charming smile.*) You're managing to keep the technical crew happy? Absolutely. (*He clicks off.*)

NIGEL *moves towards the police car.*

NIGEL (*sharp, to* KEN): Just one other small thing. That (*He touches the bonnet of the car, sharp:*) this car is it yours by any chance?

KEN (*sharp*): No it's not . . . (*Slight pause.*) It's the Chief Constable's.

NIGEL (*surprised*). It's the Chief Constable's? So we're being given the whole works. (*Polite but sharp smile.*) Do we deserve all this attention? (Ken *does not react.*) Did he really need to come?

KEN: With Festivals of this size – it's not uncommon.

NIGEL (*smiles straight at him*). Is that an example of police tact?

KEN (*uneasy*): How do you mean?

NIGEL (*moving, slight smile*). This is not *just* a festival, you know. In fact I don't like the word. We have not been using it. The whole presentation is sleeker, this occasion has rather more glitter, like the one in Paris last Spring. (*Slightly smiling.*) So this vehicle's the Chief Constable's?

LOUISE: Where is he?

KEN: I don't know. I wasn't up here when he arrived. He'll just be dropping by.

NIGEL (*sharp*): A courtesy call. (*Moving to go.*) Good . . . Good. I just like to know these things. (*He smiles at* KEN, *flicks the wing of the car.*) I'm sure you'll all behave yourselves.

Louise? Coming?

LOUISE: Of course.

LOUISE *leaves too.*
KEN *immediately moves, sharp movement, as if preoccupied. He picks up the walkie-talkie from the table, pulls out the ariel.*

KEN (*into the walkie-talkie*): Is there any sign yet? . . . (*Sharp.*) O.K. let me know.

CAROLINE (*quietly*): How long am I going to be kept here?

KEN: I'll have you moved to the incident room at the farmhouse in a moment – when I've got some men spare.

He stoops down and picks up a piece of

litter, *scrunches it up, puts it in his pocket.*

One can't put a time on these things.

CAROLINE: Am I being charged with something . . . ?

KEN *puts down the radio again on the table.*

KEN: It's not a question of one charge, it's a question of how many. Apart from everything else – you assaulted a police officer.

CAROLINE: I did not *assault* an officer – I gave him a very slight nudge when he pulled at me.

KEN: That sort of talk won't get you very far at all. (*He picks up the radio again, preoccupied _ pulls out the ariel*). Your best bet young lady is to keep as quiet as possible and answer the questions that will be put to you. And don't try to be clever when you're up there – that way you won't get yourself into even deeper water. (*He puts down the radio again.*) Count yourself lucky I told you that. (*He looks at her, sharp.*) What you got there?

CAROLINE: It's only a cough lozenge.

She is unwrapping it.

KEN (*suspicious*). A cough lozenge?

CAROLINE: Yes. (*She puts it into her mouth.*) Do you want one?

KEN: No thank you. (*Sharp.*) I rarely get ill. Pick that up. (*Indicating the small scrap of lozenge wrapping she's dropped.*)

CAROLINE *picks it up.*

KEN (*turns away from her, moves towards the table*). You've said goodbye to the rest of the concert that's certain. Girls of your age should know better, but they never do – in my experience. They're often the worst . . .

STEPHEN *enters, a young fresh faced police constable, twenty-two years old, blond hair. He walks towards* KEN.

STEPHEN: Hello sir – we're a little later than we thought.

KEN (*sharp*): I didn't know you were coming until five minutes ago.

STEPHEN: He's just dropping by. (*Genuine.*) He knew you'd like a visit.

Pause.

KEN (*sharp, impatient*): Well, where is he?

STEPHEN (*points at the car*): He's in there.

KEN (*truly surprised, staring at the car*): In there?

STEPHEN: Yes of course. He's asleep.

KEN (*staring toward the car*): Asleep! In there?

STEPHEN: He has his ten minute nap most evenings at this time, then he's all right for the rest of the night. He doesn't need much sleep.

KEN (*moving towards the car – then stops – slight laugh*): You mean he's been in there all the time.

He stares at the car, then at STEPHEN.

KEN: Come on then – aren't you going to wake him up.

STEPHEN: He wakes himself, always – it's nearly time.

KEN (*sharp grin*). His own alarm clock. Maybe he'll start using a bed when he's been Chief Constable a bit longer.

He grins at STEPHEN.

Does he sleep when you're driving him in?

STEPHEN: Sometimes (*Smiles.*) He can sleep anywhere.

KEN (*shrewd grin at STEPHEN*): Must be quite tempting for you Constable – can get away with a few things.

STEPHEN: No sir.

KEN (*staring at the car again*): So he's curled up there. (*He grins, raises his voice so KRAMER can hear.*) There's such a thing as notifying people about your arrival. It is customery.

STEPHEN *glances towards the car.*

STEPHEN (*smiles*): It should be about now.

Silence – movement in the car.

KEN: He's late.

The back door of the car opens and KRAMER gets out. He is youthful, thirty-nine, good-looking appearance. Dressed in chief constable's uniform, wearing a coat over it, and gloved hands. He talks with the traces of a south London accent.

He has an appealing smile.

KRAMER: So many smells hit one on these occasions don't they – the smell of youngsters.

As he moves towards them, he stoops down in one clean movement, picks up the remaining piece of litter, and hands it to STEPHEN.

STEPHEN (*taking it*): Sir.

KRAMER (*to KEN, smiles*): How are you then?

KEN: Everything's been very quiet so far – I've got the men well back . . .

KRAMER: Electrical supplies?

KEN: No problem.

KRAMER: First Aid?

KEN: Needed very little.

KRAMER: Noise levels . . . ?

KEN: No problems at all.

KRAMER: No complaints then.

KEN: No - not a single one yet.

KRAMER: How many toilets?

KEN (*taken aback*): Toilets? I don't know – about thirty-seven.

KRAMER (*smiles*): That's very exact Ken – thirty-seven.

KEN: In that region.

KRAMER: Usual orange one on wheels with no brakes.

KEN: Yes.

KRAMER (*glancing round, grins*): Well fastened this time, not going to run down the hill like at Westcliffe, and go through somebody's French windows? How about some tea Stephen?

STEPHEN: Yes sir, of course (*He goes over to the large metal tea urns with taps on them.*)

KRAMER (*swiftly*): Let the machine pour a little, it tastes better that way, does the grass good too.

STEPHEN *switches on the tap – tea pours out in steady stream onto the ground.*

(*Carries straight on.*) You realise mosquitoes will come up from that pond back there. (*He grins good humouredly.*)

They will . . . I'm an expert on that. At my first concert ever (*Broad smile*.) – all those years ago Ken – the DI in charge took me round with a large torch to peer at all the wildlife. We managed to see one very ill squirrel and a lot of earthworms. Who's she? (*He looks at* CAROLINE.)

KEN: She's being held.

KRAMER (*gently*): Yes I can see that. (*The tea machine is still pouring*.) You can stop it now Stephen – that's enough.

KEN: A large quantity of drugs, cannabis and cocaine, were found in a plastic bag next to her. She claims the bag is not hers. There is absolutely no identification –

CAROLINE: It isn't mine – I had no idea it was there . . .

KEN (*cutting her off*): Keep quiet. And she assaulted the officer who took her in for questioning.

CAROLINE: I did *not* assault anyone.

KRAMER (*slight smile at her interrupting*): How long's she been here? (*Looks at her*.) Been kept waiting have you? Has she been charged with anything?

KEN: Not yet. We're just moving her up to the farmhouse when I've got . . .

KRAMER (*quietly*): Do we really need that Ken – I don't think so. I don't want too many youngsters detained up there unless strictly necessary. It's a great time waster. We may well be able to clear it up out here.

KEN (*mutters*): As you like . . .

STEPHEN (*to* KRAMER): Your tea sir?

KRAMER (*takes a sip*): Jesus Christ! It's sweet, like black treacle. (*Looks at* CAROLINE, *flip*.) Have they been making you drink this . . . ?

CAROLINE: No – I haven't been offered any.

KRAMER (*to* STEPHEN *prompting him*): Give Superintendant Daniels his. One used to get really good bacon and onion sandwiches, at Festivals, soaked in fat – as big as pancakes.

STEPHEN (*up to* KEN): Yours sir.

He hands the cup to KEN *awkwardly, it's scalding hot,* KEN *drops it.*

KEN (*loud angry*): For fucks sake, be careful throwing the whole lot over me – (*Sharp*.) watch what you're doing lad!

STEPHEN (*deeply embarrassed*): Sorry sir – I thought you'd got it.

He picks the cup up.

KEN: You nearly scalded my hand off.

KRAMER (*quietly*): Its all right – be easy on the kid, he'll get you another.

KRAMER *glances towards a small pile of what looks like rubbish downstage in the corner.*

KRAMER: You been shopping Ken – what are those?

KEN: Few offensive articles that have been taken off them . . .

STEPHEN *is letting the tea machine run again.*

KRAMER (*grins*): Don't need to let it pour again Stephen. (*He looks down*.) All of these?

KEN (*looking down at the pile*): A few knives . . . ball bearings . . . usual selection. They'll have to be moved.

KRAMER (*stoops down, picks them up*): Ball bearings? – maybe the kid was an engineer? What on earth are these?

Pieces of transparent plastic with wire through them.

KEN: Those? Yes – they're sleeping pods?

KRAMER (*smiles in disbelief*): Sleeping pods – of course.

KEN (*picks one up*): Plastic stretched over wire. They pull them out like this. (*He does so*.) they have all the mod cons now you know.

KRAMER: Why've you got some?

KEN: We found them lying around . . . We didn't know what they were then. (*Indicates* CAROLINE.) She explained.

KRAMER (*glances up at her*): She explained.

He looks at a sleeping pod.

Perhaps we should try one.

He hands his tea to STEPHEN, *casually slips one leg inside.*

It's like slipping into a TRAP. You can

see straight through them.

He slips out again without effort.

KRAMER: Your turn Ken. (*To* STEPHEN): Give me my treacle back.

KEN: I don't think so.

KEN *moves to leave, turns, slight smile.*

It's not my job to tell you George, but if it goes round the Chief Constable is here, we could get a somewhat tense atmosphere. There are all kinds of riff raff down there, some darkies already throwing beer cans.

KRAMER (*polite smile*): I don't like that word Ken particularly.

KEN (*ignoring this*): You know what I mean.

KRAMER (*grins, lifts mug*): Don't worry yourself, I'm only here for the tea.

KEN *goes.*
KRAMER *glances round.*

KRAMER: Nice spot.

With an abrupt movement he feels ground with one hand, while still keeping the other hand gloved.

Yes – very dry. (*Almost without a break to* CAROLINE:) What did you say your name was?

CAROLINE (*straight at him, but rather quiet*): I didn't – am I being charged with anything?

KRAMER: What was that mumble? Get the girl a cup of tea Stephen (*to* CAROLINE:) Do you want some very sweet tea . . . ?

CAROLINE: Oh yes – if it's drinkable.

KRAMER (*patiently*): Shall we try again. What's your name?

CAROLINE (*slight smile at his patient voice*): I don't have to answer your questions – do I?

KRAMER (*amused smile*): I just want to know your name – so we can call you something.

CAROLINE: Caroline Murray.

STEPHEN *approaching with tea.*

KRAMER: Careful with that – don't pour it all over her.

STEPHEN *hands it to her gingerly.*

(*Fast:*) Has the chopper been over yet – find out – and I want an estimate on the size of the crowd, see if they've made one yet?

STEPHEN: Right sir.

He moves back to the table walkie-talkie, talks into it quietly.

KRAMER (*without a break, flicks back to* CAROLINE): What's your occupation?

CAROLINE: My occupation!

KRAMER: I think it's safe to answer that don't you.

CAROLINE: I'm a temp . . . a typist, I suppose . . . most days.

KRAMER (*smiles*): You suppose? You don't look like a typist. And where do you do your typing?

CAROLINE: Peterborough.

KRAMER (*sharp*): I once went to a Policemen's ball in Peterborough. Your boyfriend bring you here did he . . . ?

CAROLINE: No he didn't.

Slight pause

KRAMER: Then who did?

CAROLINE: Nobody (*Slight smile, quiet voice:*) I am capable you know of going to places on my own.

KRAMER (*amused smile*): Got a boyfriend?

CAROLINE: That's none of your business but no I haven't.

KRAMER: You're one of these aggressive independent girls are you? (*More formal:*) If we're both *polite* we can get along. Why did you come here?

CAROLINE: To enjoy myself . . . And you?

KRAMER (*very slight pause – then very business like*): If you don't make any noise you can stay here for a moment until we get round to you . . .

CAROLINE: What sort of noise would I make?

KRAMER (*slight smile*): A whine – (*He moves, sharp:*) do your top button up, it's come undone.

JOHN *enters, dressed all in one colour.
From a distance he looks elegant. Tightly
cropped blond hair. He is thirty-one, old
face for his age, sharp intelligent eyes, a
London accent. He talks quietly. He is
holding a book in one hand. He stops
when he sees* KRAMER *and stands very
still.*

KRAMER: Who are you?

JOHN (*surprised smile on his face, repeats it
quietly*): Who am I?

He stares straight at KRAMER *for a
moment, then he moves sharply towards
table, hostile manner.*

Just a technician come to check the place
over.

STEPHEN (*moving close to* KRAMER):
He's a singer, Sir.

KRAMER (*watching* JOHN, *in his plain
nondescript clothes*): A singer? Are you
sure?

STEPHEN: He's one of the stars.

JOHN (*picking up a very large glass jug of
tomato juice, from a small side table,
beside the main covered table*): One of the
artistes.

*He downs the tomato juice in one,
incredibly thirsty, immediately pours
another.*

JOHN (*sharp, at* KRAMER): I think this is
our paddock. Our private place, away
from the trash behind the stage, there are
other places like this for the smaller fry.
(*He smiles to himself, self-mocking.*) Such
as my support band.

KRAMER (*to* STEPHEN): You recognise
him?

STEPHEN: Yes Sir.

JOHN *empties the second glass.*
STEPHEN *moves back up next to*
CAROLINE.

KRAMER: What's your name?

JOHN (*with his back to them, immediately
pouring himself a third glass*): John. (*With
his back to* KRAMER:) And you look
rather like the local constabulary. They
seem to be everywhere.

*He slips a couple of pills into his mouth
and swills them down.*

You probably didn't notice but I've just
been performing.

KRAMER: I'm afraid I wasn't here.

JOHN (*looks upstage to where
CAROLINE is, loud*): There seems to be
a girl over there.

JOHN *stares at her for a second.*

KRAMER: Yes.

JOHN *suddenly moves sharply and pulls
off his T-shirt, he is wearing another
identical T-shirt underneath.*

JOHN (*sharp*): You're not meant to see this
really but it can't be helped.

*He peels off a second T-shirt, and then a
third, each identical, tearing them off with
obvious relief.*

(*Wringing the T-shirts out*): They are
soaked.

He pulls of a fourth.

You look surprised.

KRAMER: Do you play like that?

JOHN: It is to make me sweat on stage. (*He
takes another off. Flip:*) There are twenty-
six layers of this, only half have come off.
(*Dropping T-shirt.*) You can have them if
you like. (*Dead pan.*) It's hard work, you
know.

Takes another drink of tomato juice.

What are you staring at?

KRAMER (*watching him closely*): Do I
know your music?

JOHN (*smile*): Are you referring to what I
do as music?

KRAMER: Name some tunes.

JOHN (*amused smile*): Name some tunes.
I don't think so. They're really not very
interesting. Fairly middle of the road
stuff, for driving home on the motorway
really. My child of six likes them but then
he doesn't drive. He failed his test last
month. (*Sharp grin, indicating
KRAMER:*) He thinks I'm joking.

*He sips tomato juice as he stares at
KRAMER.*

(*Straight at* KRAMER:) When I first saw
people drink this stuff – when I was small,
I thought they were drinking blood. I
really did.

KRAMER: Maybe they were.

JOHN (*quiet smile*): Maybe I am now.

Then he laughs. Pause.

KRAMER: Lot of people out there, are there?

JOHN: Quite a few. More than enough. It's a big occasion (*Sharp staring at him.*) Haven't you got a programme?

JOHN *produces one from his back pocket.*

It's more of a brochure, goes with the glossiness of the occasion (*Glancing down at the programme.*) Starts modestly enough, 'The Party' – and then 'A celebratory extravaganza plus magnificent laser show'. He's throwing in everything he could get across the whole musical spectrum, and not just music, there's a lot of expensive hardware here (*Slight smile.*) far removed from the broken glass and bare feet occasions, thank Christ. (*Produces a special pass.*) See, you can tell even with this, the special pass is waterproof, and unbreakable, and has a luminous rim all the way round so it can be found in the dark. (*At* KRAMER:) Thoughtful, don't you think? (*Hands* KRAMER *the programme.*) Here, you should read it. He's the second Gatsby, our host. Didn't you know that?

He looks straight at KRAMER, *sees he doesn't understand.*

Never mind. (JOHN *moves.*) He chose the right night.

He glances over his shoulder.

The man in the white suit throwing his big party – I wonder where he is?

KRAMER (*watching* JOHN *fascinated*): What's the book?

JOHN (*stares at him*): The curiosity of the police. Insatiable isn't it. An incurable disease. (*He hands it to* KRAMER.) Wondering if it's hollow?

KRAMER *opens the book.*

JOHN: It's Browning.

KRAMER (*looking at the book*): Poetry.

JOHN: Right first time. I read him a lot. (*Flip:*) 'Robert and Elizabeth' is my favourite musical. (*He grins at*

KRAMER.) I went to it the night I got engaged.

LOUISE *enters,* JOHN *is by the table.*

LOUISE (*glancing at* JOHN *by the table*): So you found it. (*Then she sees* KRAMER.) Who are you?

KRAMER: My name's George Kramer.

LOUISE (*she smiles at him*): Of course – you're paying your courtesy call. (*She immediately turns her back to him and moves to* JOHN.) You were very good. (*Smiling.*) You finished two minutes early, you know, according to the others.

JOHN (*mock*): Impossible.

LOUISE: I've just been taking a look at the audience. They're dressed in roughly three different styles.

JOHN (*dead pan*): As many as that.

LOUISE: A sort of unfussy, drab non-committal look which is most of them, then the stylish ones, the new chic, kids in suits and well cut clothes which is quite a few of them. And then little outcrops of outrageousness. (*Opening her hand, confidentially excluding* KRAMER.) You'll never believe this but look – (*Her hand's full of hair.*) – I just walked past a group of three people sitting by a gorse bush – and they all had liquorice in their hair, their heads were covered with it. I asked if I could cut some off and keep it.

JOHN (*looking at her*): Complete madmen. Let's see. (*He feels it.*)

LOUISE: It's so ugly. He had lovely blond hair, a great mane of it, but it was all mixed in with strands of liquorice. He said he's washed it in a hot basinful (*Shiver of revulsion.*) I don't know how they can do it.

JOHN: I wonder if it hurts them. (*Holds hair up.*) Do they chew it in tea-breaks do you think?

LOUISE: I don't know if its a new, bizarre fashion, or just kids having a bit of fun.

KRAMER *is watching them.*

LOUISE (*leaning close to* JOHN, *but audible*): Has he been here long?

KRAMER (*to* STEPHEN): Try to get Ken, I want another word with him.

LOUISE (*turns and looks straight at*

KRAMER): So the car belongs to you . . .

KRAMER (*slight smile*): This is the car I use, yes, Madam.

LOUISE (*moving towards the car*): I've always been afraid to go near police cars. You expect to get sucked into them.

JOHN (*caustic smile*): You've never been in trouble with the police in your life – hooligan days in the grime of Mayfair or wherever you live, they've never ever touched you.

LOUISE (*at him*): You're still coming down from your act, aren't you? (*Slight smile.*) So I'll ignore that.

JOHN: And the money! What was it your husband's father did? Invent the gramophone?

LOUISE: No – the automatic turntable on your record-player.

JOHN: Earned him a million pounds before breakfast every day of the year.

LOUISE: Yes but then it was a rather good idea. (*She is up to the police car staring through the window.*) There are lots of clothes inside here – nearly a whole wardrobe – that's unexpected. And slippers. (*She looks at the gleaming metal of the car.*) You keep it very clean don't you? You can see yourself in it.

KRAMER (*indicating* STEPHEN): The kid here gives it a good polish every morning.

LOUISE (*touching the side of the car*): He did all this. Does he polish your buttons as well? (*Looks at him.*)

KRAMER: No they look after themselves.

LOUISE: I read somewhere that policemen are window cleaners in their spare time because of their pay.

KRAMER (*sharp*): No police officer in the county does any moonlighting, ever.

LOUISE (*straight at him*): I am sorry I have offended you. Can I? (*She lifts the camera to take a picture. Focussing the camera.*) Is one allowed to take photos of the police, or does one have to write to some department asking permission?

KRAMER *is taken aback at her suddenly pointing the camera at him.*

KRAMER: No permission is required

(*Slight smile.*) in normal circumstances.

LOUISE: And what are these? Try to keep still!

KRAMER (*uneasy*): I'd prefer it if you didn't take a picture.

LOUISE (*camera turned on him*): Just try to keep still. No that's awful, relax. You don't like being photographed do you?

KRAMER: I don't mind either way. I wasn't expecting it.

LOUISE: You needn't worry these are only for me. They won't be spreading through the newspapers tomorrow. Relax.

She takes a picture and keeps the camera trained on him.

I just passed some police back there. They look very good in their short sleeves and blue shirts, with just a little flesh poking through, and their red cheeks . . . That's better.

She's taking pictures all the time.

Just like the village policeman in British films. They looked really young flopped in the long grass (*She smiles.*) keeping out of the way. (*She turns away from him – then glances back.*) My husband who you haven't met yet – he's got everything you can think of lined up for all these people tonight and he doesn't want any trouble.

NIGEL *enters in his white suit, he stands looking at them all.*

NIGEL: You're all here. (*Glances at* KRAMER.) I'm Nigel Richards. Don't worry, I know who you are.

KRAMER: George Kramer.

NIGEL: Precisely, (*Turning from him.*) glad you could come. (*Moving to* JOHN.) Very speedy, I thought, up there. It was rather good.

JOHN (*slight smile*): It was O.K. It was quite painless really.

NIGEL: And you came in on schedule. There's a car standing by if you want one. (*Indicating the Police car.*) Not that one.

NIGEL *is by* JOHN *and* LOUISE *away from the Police.*

You look rather different from when I saw you before.

JOHN: Possibly. Every nine months I kind

of transform. One must keep up with the times.

NIGEL *whispers knowingly to* JOHN *and* LOUISE, *indicating the police.*

NIGEL: Seems a little fraternisation is expected of us. It's amazing how they go straight to the food, invariably. I wasn't sure where you'd gone.

LOUISE (*slight smile*): You weren't meant to.

NIGEL (*moves, smiles; into walkie-talkie*): OK, keep it low and unobtrusive. Yes – till they come. (*Charming smile.*) Try to keep the North Gate closed, I don't think that should be beyond those grotesque heavies we hired. The Hulks. Quite. (*Knowing smile.*) That doesn't surprise me one bit . . . (*He smiles charmingly.*) I don't think we'd better go on with this conversation tempting though it is . . . OK, call me at once, as soon as they arrive . . . (*He clicks off the machine.*)

Simon's proving right, he's a good neutral personality, his announcements are really inocuous. And he can even pronounce his 'R's'.

KRAMER (*who has been watching him*): How much is all this costing you?

Surprised pause.

NIGEL (*looks up, amused smile*): I didn't quite – could you repeat that?

KRAMER: How much is this whole jamboree costing you?

NIGEL (*glances at* LOUISE): A very full frontal question. (*Pause.*) How much do you think? Have a guess.

KRAMER: I can't. I don't know how these things operate.

NIGEL (*slight smile, staring at* KRAMER): Go on, try. Have a guess.

KRAMER *doesn't move.*

It's costing me £450 per minute. Or to put it more graphically, 7½ of these (*He flicks out pound notes.*) are pouring out of our pocket every second; (*He clicks his fingers casually.*) if we go into overtime it becomes £35 a second, and then of course there's golden time . . . An event like this does not come cheap. (*Smiles.*) A party of this size. Especially as it's not just bands I'm presenting, but the risk is minimal,

one has rights on the album of tonight, the video recording and there's even a little advertising around the place. Life insurance (*Turns to* JOHN.) I even have one of these meters from America telling you how much money you've spent as the evening goes on – like a taxi meter. It gives off a warning bleep. You're meant to take it out in private (*He slips out the meter.*) and have an agonised look . . .

KRAMER: And you do?

NIGEL (*suddenly swings*): DON'T TOUCH THE TABLE.

KRAMER: I was just (*He is holding a small table decoration that he has picked up from the cover.*)

NIGEL (*steelily polite smile*): Have you broken that?

KRAMER (*looking down*): I don't think so.

NIGEL (*sharp*): Please don't touch anything.

KRAMER *puts it down.*

It may look like an ordinary table but it's no such thing.

KRAMER (*standing at the covers*): What's wrong with it?

NIGEL: I will demonstrate something to you. (*He moves.*) You may find this educational. (*Quick glance at* LOUISE, *then he moves closer to the table. Dryly.*) You must watch this carefully – very few people are allowed to see this.

He slowly pulls back the muslin cover, to reveal an extraordinary display; a whole table length of shimmering goods on the white table cloth: silver plates, food, drinks, tall candlesticks, other table decorations. The table is the length of the stage and the impression is sumptousness.

A moment's silence.

KRAMER (*staring at it*): It's quite impressive. A very generous spread.

NIGEL (*sharp smile*): Generosity had nothing to do with it.

NIGEL *walks along the side of his table.*

This all has to be provided. They demand it – it is an essential part of tonight. (*Slight smile.*) People have been known not to perform because the cream has been off in a single eclair.

JOHN: *I've* done that. Not often, but I've done it.

NIGEL: All this catering had to be done by those Italians in Camden Passage and they charge exhorbitantly of course. (*Smiles.*) This table is one of the most important features of tonight. (*Indicating* KRAMER.) I don't think he believes me.

KRAMER (*quiet*): Not for a minute.

NIGEL: You see those things down there that look like menus (*They are hanging at the end of the table.*) Those are the contracts. Immediately available for both parties in case of dispute. Go on, you can have a look at them.

KRAMER *looks at them.*

They have minions especially employed solely to think up more and more improbable demands for them, to make it as hard as possible for anybody to get them on stage. They're very reluctant to perform live anymore. (*Dry smile.*) It becomes an assault course – which one has to win.

LOUISE: Right.

NIGEL (*abruptly to* KRAMER): Look at the table.

KRAMER: I've looked. I've never seen a table with so much food on it, it's almost sagging under the weight.

NIGEL (*he smiles*): It's *not just food.* Look again, between the seafood in aspic and the highland patés, which are very good by the way, you'll see some curious things – gold earrings and handmade tooth-brushes and books on Alfred Hitchcock. And look under the table, what do you see?

KRAMER: Boxes.

NIGEL: Pull them out.

KRAMER *does so.*

The usual assortment of portable tele-visions and cassette recorders that we have to give them in addition to their fee, but the catch of course is that they have to be of a very obscure make, Finnish or Hungarian or Javan. Like the new 4" T.V. screens in the shape of a wristwatch. They're not stupid, everything is chosen simply for its maximum nuisance value.

(*He looks down at the table.*) I have my own people scouring London for it all.

Most of this is of course for our Main Act, the rest is for him (*Indicating* JOHN.) and the new phenomenon Mister David, you know this new wonder person; he's been especially hard to please. Seemingly endless phone calls with his agent but he is of course very hot at the moment, very recent. But he certainly made a lot of demands.

JOHN: I think you've got off lightly.

NIGEL: Of course I have. I haven't had to provide anything illegal for a start. (*Charming smile at* KRAMER. *By the table:*) I have only had to provide all of this (*He looks at table.*) every item has been double checked.

LOUISE: And they may just have one slight nibble and then leave the lot. Until then we can't even pick at it, except for him. (*Indicating* JOHN.)

NIGEL (*indicating* JOHN): Fortunately he's performed already.

JOHN (*moving over to table, slight smile*): But if he wishes he can suddenly turn nasty and refuse rights on the album being made of tonight.

NIGEL (*taken aback, then sharp smile*): He could. But he won't.

JOHN *is by the table, he grins.*

JOHN (*smiling*): I'm afraid . . . I don't see any French mustard. (*Pause. They all stare.*) You can breathe again, I've found it.

NIGEL (*moving the muslin cover back, slowly covering the table*): It is rather pretty, it has to be said.

LOUISE: And we can't touch any of it.

NIGEL (*sharp smile*): It's like my offerings to a hostile tribe.

The table is covered.

Of course it has to be nailed to the ground – so stray bullocks and policemen can't cause havoc.

LOUISE (*smiles*): Or anyone else.

NIGEL (*straight at* KRAMER): I don't think they'll mind the police car being here, they might quite like that. And I don't mind it either, particularly. (*Slight smile.*) It's the police they may object to. (*Watching* KRAMER.) I've been watching the progress of your tea cup.

KRAMER (*sipping tea*): You don't have to worry, I'm only passing. Nobody will know I'm here. (*He grins.*) I won't raise my head above the parapet.

KRAMER *turns,* KEN *is entering holding a bloated sleeping bag. It is bright evening light.*

KRAMER: We thought we'd lost you Ken – as you can see we have company now. What's that you got?

KEN: It's a sleeping bag case.

KRAMER (*grins*): I would never have guessed. Adding it to your collection?

NIGEL: We're not planning to go on that late.

KEN: A constable handed it to me.

KRAMER (*quiet smile*): Why bring it up here?

KEN: Because it appears to be addressed to you – and I know . . .

KRAMER (*surprised*): Addressed to me?

NIGEL *sideways smile to* LOUISE *and* JOHN.

KEN (*reads the message off the side*): To the chief constable then a couple of obscenities and something I can't read.

JOHN (*slight smile*): I don't think we want any filth up here.

KEN: Thought you'd like to see it George.

KRAMER (*taking the sleeping bag*): Does it say who it's from?

KEN: No.

NIGEL (*sharp smile*): I believe we're seeing an actual piece of real police business.

KRAMER (*holding the bag*): It's very heavy and warm like they've just been sleeping in it. (*He turns bag over.*) There's something else written here.

KEN (*surprised*): Is there? – I hadn't noticed.

KRAMER: It reads (*He reads:*) 'This is going to *go off.*'

LOUISE *looks round.*

LOUISE (*smiling at him*): Perhaps – you

should put it down and not wave it around.

JOHN (*watching the bag*): I think I might meander off.

But he doesn't move.

NIGEL (*sharp*): Do you think this is our statutory bomb hoax. (*Sharp smile to* KRAMER.) Obligingly brought straight to us.

KRAMER: This is not a bomb, otherwise Superintendent Daniels would not have brought it here.

NIGEL (*smiles*): One hopes so.

LOUISE *and* NIGEL *and* JOHN *though almost completely certain it is a joke, begin to move rather apprehensively.*

LOUISE: Perhaps we should leave them to do their job in peace, not cramp their style.

NIGEL (*quiet smile*): I take it they know what they're doing.

LOUISE (*staring at the sleeping bag*): What happens if . . . (*Nervous smile.*) . . . just supposing . . . just for the sake of argument you're wrong.

KRAMER *unzips the bag, milk gushes out onto the stage.*

KRAMER (*slight smile as it pours out*): A milk bomb – several goatsfull. (*He peers.*) I think there's a little yoghurt at the bottom. (*To* KEN:) I don't think we need evacuate the place.

JOHN (*laughing to himself*): 'Could go off'.

KEN: Just an idiotic prank.

NIGEL (*to* KRAMER): Sent to you, I think.

JOHN (*prodding it slightly with his foot*): They used to use these, you know (*Slight pause.*) for other reasons.

LOUISE (*quiet*): I really can't stand practical jokes, and people just love playing them.

KRAMER (*picking up the bag, tossing it to the side of the table*): Quite a clever hoax. Can't arrest them because the word bomb was never mentioned, but it still made me wonder for a millimetre of a second. (*He glances upstage at* CAROLINE.) Perhaps it's hers.

CAROLINE (*looking back at him*): I've

never seen something like that before . . .

JOHN (*coming up behind* LOUISE): Allow me – there's a red centipede in your hair (*Poking at her hair.*) won't take a second I'll . . .

LOUISE: Where? (*She moves her head and shakes it.*) Where is it?

JOHN: No, no, wait, otherwise it will get stuck.

LOUISE (*shaking her head even more vigorously*): Stuck? Where is it? (*She sees him smiling. Slight laugh.*) Please don't do that – I always believe things like that and I don't like them. People at parties, pulling cashew nuts out of your ears, things like that. I must remember not to stand near you if that's what's going to happen.

NIGEL's *radio has been buzzing, he has taken it out and is listening to it centre stage.*

NIGEL: O.K. yes. (*His voice sharp:*) Really? You're sure? That's interesting. No, no, keep it as before. I'll come back to you. (*He looks up, sharp smile.*) They're going to be late. *An hour late.* (*Sideways glance at the meter.*) Which is good news of course, perverse though it may seem, it means they're on their way. Just have to change the programme.

LOUISE (*smiles to herself*): A reschedule.

Pause. NIGEL *moves.*

KRAMER: Why don't you play your light show now . . .

NIGEL *glances up surprised at* KRAMER's *intervention.*

NIGEL: You've heard about that . . . I am in fact holding it in reserve for later. (*He glances up.*) and it should be darker.

KRAMER: You've got to give them something haven't you? (*Smiles.*) It'll show up crystal sharp.

NIGEL (*slight pause and looking at* KRAMER): Thank you. Actually – as it just happens – there is some nice bloated cloud above at the moment for the first time. You need cloud, do you realise, otherwise you wouldn't be able to see it, on a summer night like this. (*Then a sharp movement into the walkie-talkie.*) Simon prepare lasers to go in 2½ minutes. I've

decided. No they'll show well on the cloud . . . as planned (*Knowing grin.*) Are they still coming through the turnstiles? The punters. Yes, I know there aren't any turnstiles, I was speaking figuratively, through the wire. (*Louder.*) The fence. Hurry them up.

KEN (*into his own walkie-talkie*): Prepare for the light show. It will be coming from behind the stage. Keep men where they are.

KRAMER (*looks upstage at* CAROLINE): Just getting round to you. Your nose is running.

CAROLINE: Is it? I haven't got a handker-chief. It was confiscated.

KRAMER: That I don't believe. Here you can borrow one of mine. (*Pulls out new white handkerchief and hands it to* STEPHEN *who hands it to* CAROLINE.) It's clean, you needn't worry, uncontaminated.

KRAMER *watches her for a second.*

NIGEL (*into the walkie-talkie*): Excellent. As soon as you're ready. (*He clicks off the machine dryly.*) The party's underway again, they didn't have to wait long.

He pulls out a long brown cigarette.

They send you out a rather large catalogue, the laser firms, choose what you want for up there, like choosing wall-paper. Then you go to a rather large warehouse in the trendy part of dockland. Originally I thought of making the whole night one giant laser show.

LOUISE (*by* NIGEL): They're very strange looking things, the actual machines, like very thin coffins. And a man sits at the computer that controls them and presses buttons like playing a key board. There's something very odd about it.

During the speeches LOUISE *moves slowly upstage, apart from the others.*

NIGEL (*standing up centre stage in his white suit*): We haven't begun to see what can be done with them yet. It's as primitive as the early days of flying. Soon whole films will be able to be made out of them, and projected in the sky (*Smiles.*) the last word in cinerama, the widest cinemascope there's ever been in fact.

CBS has already poured millions into it. They're developing so fast, the technology, it's difficult to keep track. New things become available all the time. You'll be able to show a whole city a film at the same time and pay for it by advertising. Rather large coca-cola cans hanging over London in 3D; the size of St. Pauls probably. One summer night, just like this, one can imagine it, colossal car chases and battle scenes up there – with people sitting on their own balconies drinking it in. One should be able to make a whole city catch its breath at the same time. (*He looks up.*) What you're about to see, this is just a trailer.

KRAMER (*looking up too*): I like a bit of spectacle, a bit of circus in the sky – these lasers I've often thought about them coming into town on the motorway . . .

Pause, they look at him in surprise.

NIGEL: Really?

JOHN (*quiet smile*): Just think what one could do. Drive people mad with no trouble at all. Vast pornographic parts hanging in the sky over Tunbridge Wells for instance, everywhere you looked, there they would be, the tits just scraping the tops of the houses. You could never get away. I must remember to take one home with me tonight.

NIGEL (*into the walkie-talkie*): Fine. Any second! Looking forward to it. (*Dry smile.*) And I hope they are too. (*He clicks off.*)

The distant sound of an announcement.
LOUISE *upstage.*

KEN (*to KRAMER, slight smile*): I remember the fireworks on V.E. night, still the best night of my life, been downhill ever since! They were all red white and blue, most of the kids here weren't even born which is their loss. It was a cracking summer night much warmer than this one. (*Sudden shrewd look at KRAMER.*) You're probably much too young to remember, George. You must have been in bed.

LOUISE *moving nearer.*

KRAMER: Not quite Ken, almost but not quite. I can remember everything from the age of five months.

LOUISE (*suddenly lets out a real shout*):

Ough!

They all turn and stare at her upstage and as they do so she lifts her camera and takes a flash.

Good. (*She laughs, they all stare at her.*) Portrait of startled people. Keep it still – again. (*They all stare at her, she smiles.*) You do look rather bizarre (*Takes another flash.*) No. Just hold it one more moment.

NIGEL (*smiles*): Louise – what are you doing? Where were you sliding off to?

LOUISE: Nowhere, (*Slight pause.*) just avoiding the mosquitoes.

NIGEL (*sharp*): Come on, come back here. (*Moderating his tone.*) Or you'll miss it.

LOUISE (*smiles*): Of course. (*She moves downstage to join them. She looks up.*) Up there. If you point a camera at them does anything come out at all, or does it cause some strange chemical reaction and break the lense.

NIGEL (*tolerant smile*): You don't begin to understand, do you, how they work.

LOUISE (*gently*): No, of course not, (*Pause.*) and do you?

NIGEL (*more tenderly*): You ought to enjoy yourself tonight – it is partly for you after all. (*Lowering his voice, lightly.*) Where were you really going just now?

Music starts, something stirring.

LOUISE (*slight smile*): I told you, nowhere – in particular.

KRAMER: What are we going to see first?

NIGEL (*smiling, sipping from his glass*): An official surpise. You can try guessing of course.

LOUISE (*staring up*): It's a red cow.

KRAMER: A red cow?

NIGEL: Then practically everything you can think of will follow. A giant hypodermic needle. An orchid, a girl's breast, a vast pair of gym shoes. (*He stretches out his arm.*)

The music changes now. He flicks his finger as the music changes into jazzy rock. A still moment as they stand for a second waiting and the music gets louder, then a very bright red light bursts across the stage. Pause.

NIGEL (*looking around him, sharply, but not at all panicky*): I think . . . (*He spins round.*) I do believe . . . yes . . . (*Sharp but confident.*) the bloody idiots are pointing it at us.

JOHN: Yes they are.

NIGEL: I think you better get down everyone to be safe. (*Then sharp.*) Come on get down on the ground.

LOUISE: What, right down? Okay.

They lie down – LOUISE, JOHN, STEPHEN, KEN, NIGEL, CAROLINE, *lying on their stomachs.* LOUISE *is in her evening dress.*

KRAMER (*remaining standing*): No, you don't have to.

NIGEL: Where's the radio? (*He picks it up sharp and still urbane, not losing control.*) Now listen you morons – you're pointing it at *us.* (*Really sharp.*) Do you think it's beyond you to get them to switch it off.

LOUISE (*calmly*): I hope we're not going to catch fire.

NIGEL (*flicking it off*): This is ludicrous. (*To* KRAMER.) I should get down if I were you – it can blind you.

KRAMER: Not at this range it can't.

NIGEL: Do as you wish. (*Into the walkie-talkie.*) Now come on Simon – move it.

KRAMER (*slight smile*): You mean we've got part of the udder of a thousand foot cow on us at the moment? (*Then to* CAROLINE:) You can stand up, it's perfectly safe. It's just like a very bright torch.

NIGEL (*very sharp*): Simon – I will only say it once more. Get it OFF.

The red light clicks off, leaving the late evening.

(*Amused smile.*) You can get up now. It's safe. (*He stands up.*) We hope . . .

They all get up.

LOUISE: Surprised it hasn't burnt the grass.

NIGEL (*smiling to* JOHN): They obviously haven't found the right line yet.

JOHN: You mean they're going to get more accurate?

Suddenly they all laugh. LOUISE, NIGEL *and* JOHN *grouped together.*

NIGEL: The idiots, what are we paying them for.

JOHN (*smiling, nods*): Nearly exterminated a distinguished career.

NIGEL (*laughing*): Probably manage to point it at themselves next time.

LOUISE (*lightly*): I told you that they were slightly frightening. (*She laughs.*) I wonder if anyone saw us, spread all over the ground.

NIGEL (*grins*): They may be about to strike again.

KRAMER (*to* NIGEL): They mustn't be used again until they've been totally re-checked and retested.

NIGEL (*looks up, politely hostile*): Quite. Thank you.

KEN (*mumbling into the walkie-talkie*): Check laser equipment in vicinity of stage.

NIGEL (*into his own walkie-talkie*): Simon – don't let them try again until we come down to supervise things. We can't use them if they're unsafe (*Charming smile.*) Is that clearly understood – we don't want holes burnt in us particularly.

LOUISE: Right. After all they're only tricks of the light. We haven't all changed colour have we? (*She looks down at her dress.*)

The arc lights click on – a mixture of evening light and the sharp light of the arc lights.

LOUISE (*startled*): What's that?

KRAMER: Just the arc lights, must be on a time switch madam.

LOUISE (*to* KRAMER): Thank you. (*Sharp.*) I might not have worked that out for myself. (*She moves, slight smile.*) I think I'm getting away from here until it's been declared safe.

JOHN: You're right. (*As* LOUISE *passes* JOHN:) Wait. You really have got something in your hair. Let me –

LOUISE (*embarrassed laugh*): Could you, please, just, not . . . I asked you not to, okay.

JOHN: No, let me. (*He pulls something out of her hair.*) You see. I've got it. It's wriggling. (*He shows it to her.*) Sometimes I'm telling the truth.

LOUISE (*looks at him sharply*): Yes, possibly. I'm not at all sure, though. (*She goes.*)

JOHN: I'll come with you (*He glances towards* KRAMER.) maybe more peaceful. (*He goes.*)

NIGEL: I need to find Mister David now. He'll have to go on right now. He was meant to go on between the two sets of our main act and artistes hate being rescheduled (*He looks at* KRAMER, *steelily polite.*) I don't want to sound unreasonable – particularly, but I think it might be easier if you keep your advice to yourself – while you're still here.

KRAMER: I was just . . .

NIGEL (*sharply, cutting him off*): OK? I would appreciate that! (*He moves to go, more dangerous:*) I hope that is understood. (*He goes sharply.*)

KRAMER (*immediately turns to* KEN): Ken, will you go down there and keep an eye on them, nobody's to flick any sort of switch until it's declared safe.

KEN (*resentful at being ordered*): YES – I was about to do just that. (*Split second pause.*) You don't think George you . . .

KRAMER (*slight smile, cutting him off*): No, I don't think so.

KEN (*moves slightly*): I hope you know what you're doing George. (*He looks at* CAROLINE, *loud.*) Must do something about that girl – I'll call the drug squad up to fetch her.

KEN *moves towards the exit.*

KRAMER (*as* KEN *is at the exit*): I saw you bowling last week – 3 for 28 wasn't it?

KEN (*very surprised*): I didn't see you there . . .

KRAMER: I was just passing. I saw you from the car. Your runs up got shorter.

KEN *goes.* KRAMER *watches him go for a split second then swings round.*

Stephen, we're staying!

He moves, his adrenalin really flowing.

We're staying at the party for a while.

STEPHEN *is standing upstage deeply concerned.*

(*Loud:*) Stephen?

STEPHEN (*head flicks back*): Sorry sir – I was just thinking . . .

KRAMER: Do that later in private – what's the matter with you tonight . . .

STEPHEN: Nothing sir – at all. (*He smiles.*) Talk to us like servants, don't they, sir.

KRAMER (*grins*): I hardly notice it anymore; my first ever job out of training school, a mayor's banquet, I was standing at the foot of the stairs, and all the ladies of the town, in their leopard skin coats, and totally soaked in scent, kept on hitting me as they brushed past on their way up, like I was a polystyrene model – *they never looked at you at all;* one of them even managed to cut me with the top of her handbag . . .

STEPHEN *giggles.*

(*Sharp, fast:*) Radio back to Clare Street from the car and get an availability check on the chopper – I want it over before it gets really dark, and make sure it's not that red-haired maniac with half his teeth missing at the controls – we don't want anyone decapitated . . .

STEPHEN *goes to the car and shuts the door, driving seat.* KRAMER *swings round, his manner sharp, alert, alone on stage with* CAROLINE.

How old are you?

CAROLINE (*who is on the other side of the stage from him, looks up*): Those drugs were absolutely nothing to do with me, so can I go now?

KRAMER (*smiles, ignoring this*): You don't have to answer any questions if you don't want to – how old are you?

CAROLINE (*watching him carefully*): I'm twenty-four – (*Slight pause.*) and a half . . .

KRAMER *staring at her across the whole width of the stage.*

KRAMER: Really? You look younger.

CAROLINE (*slight smile*): Thank you . . .

KRAMER: You see – you like being told that, despite all this ladies Lib . . .

CAROLINE (*ignoring this*): Can I stand up?

KRAMER: Of course, you're not chained to the tree are you?

CAROLINE (*slight smile*): Not yet.

CAROLINE *gets up,* KRAMER, *in a very detached way, watching her do so.*

KRAMER: How much do you weigh?

CAROLINE: Weigh? My weight . . .

KRAMER: I'm very good at judging people's weight. (*Split second pause as he judges.*) Eight stone three. How many pounds am I out then?

CAROLINE (*impressed, surprised*): Just two . . .

KRAMER (*slight grin*): If you tidied yourself up, you'd be quite presentable. You bite your nails.

CAROLINE: Yes – I'd noticed that for myself (*Smiles.*) is that why I'm being held here . . . ?

Slight tense pause.

KRAMER (*very matter of fact*): Despite your quiet little voice, you're rather a cheeky kid aren't you – not afraid to open your mouth.

CAROLINE (*quiet, staring across*): Am I meant to call you sir.

KRAMER: No, Mr Kramer will do. You've probably never spoken to a policeman before except to ask him for the time . . .

CAROLINE (*slight smile*): Are you trying to find out if I've been in trouble before?

KRAMER (*glances towards car*): Stephen – come on! (*Turns back to her immediately.*) Look after you well in Peterborough do they? What on earth do you find to do there . . .

CAROLINE: You ask very odd questions . . . I read a lot. I do evening classes in French.

KRAMER: Evening classes. (*Slight smile.*) Typing is not enough then.

CAROLINE: Would *you* like to type all day?

KRAMER: In the past I've often had to.

CAROLINE: I'm certainly not going to spend the rest of my life doing it –

(*Smiles.*) I mean to make sure of that.

KRAMER: Should get yourself a reasonably priced husband – settle down.

CAROLINE (*looks up slight smile*): I don't think that's even worth answering.

KRAMER: Tonight I'm the judge of that.

She stares at him across the stage.

And what about all these many boy-friends you haven't mentioned . . . ?

CAROLINE (*very slight pause*): I lived with someone for a long time – not that it's anything to do with you.

KRAMER (*slight smile*): No. Treat you well, did he?

CAROLINE: Not very, no. (*Pointed, at him:*) I spent my time in one room becoming more and more grey, I got fat and very lethargic. I hardly ever spoke, just made noises and cooked. (*Looking at him.*): This is probably going down in some file as I speak. Instantly taped.

KRAMER (*slight smile*): Don't worry, I'll erase it.

CAROLINE: I'm very independent now – and I'm going to teach I hope.

KRAMER (*watching her*): So that's why you've been hitting police officers and carrying drugs on this glittering occasion.

CAROLINE: But I haven't . . . (*Quiet:*) and you believe me don't you . . . (*No reaction.*) or are you going to send me up to the farmhouse and have it coaxed out of me. (*She smiles, quiet.*) Do they hit people up there?

KRAMER: Nobody in my county ever lays a finger on detained persons. I've made sure of that. I will not tolerate boorish men in my force – or boorish women. (*He smiles.*) So we would have problems employing you. (*Staring at her.*) I have a daughter – much younger than you of course. (*Matter of fact, watching her.*) Some girls still flop around the house in their mother's slippers and helping make the marmalade sandwiches for tea. Others are writhing in the discos at the age of ten.

CAROLINE: Why you here?

KRAMER: It's why *you're* here that we're concerned with.

CAROLINE: I mean a Chief Constable must have better things to do . . .

KRAMER (*slight laugh*): Than what?

CAROLINE (*smiles*): Than make a nuisance of himself here – probably cause trouble . . .

Split second pause.

KRAMER (*firm, louder*): Don't get too cheeky young lady, you're being questioned in connection with a crime . . .

Very slight pause, he watches her.

Nobody knows I'm here.

CAROLINE (*staring back*): Have you always been a policeman?

KRAMER (*he smiles*): Always! Yes. I was born wearing navy blue nappies.

CAROLINE: You seem a little different – to other policemen.

KRAMER (*he smiles at her*): That's purely accidental. (*Looks at her.*) I once thought of being a trapeze artist.

The siren in the police car goes off, loud, pounding.

(*He swings round, startled.*) Switch that thing OFF! (*The siren continues, KRAMER raises his voice:*) Stephen – stop that . . .

It stops. Silence.

(*Sharp, authorative.*) Stephen?

The car door opens slowly, STEPHEN emerges sheepishly.

STEPHEN: Sorry sir . . . my hand slipped . . . and it sort of went off.

KRAMER: That will have gone out across the entire place . . . just what we didn't need. (*Calm.*) What on earth's the matter with you . . . ?

STEPHEN: Nothing – I'm just being clumsy tonight sir . . .

KRAMER: I don't like inefficiency . . .

STEPHEN: I know that sir.

Distant shout rings out and a spatter of distant applause.

KRAMER (*glancing in its direction*): There you are . . . (*He glances back at STEPHEN.*) Come here.

STEPHEN *obediently moves up to him.*

Is it your wife again?

STEPHEN: My wife. (*Smiles nervously.*) What about her sir?

KRAMER: Not waiting up for you is she . . . ?

STEPHEN: Waiting up? No. (*Slight nervous giggle.*) She'll be in bed . . .

KRAMER: Only a kid isn't she.

STEPHEN: Yes. (*Impressed.*) How do you remember that?

KRAMER: About nineteen – and a little thing, not very high?

He holds his hand about 4½ feet above the ground.

STEPHEN: Yes, that's right – she's only nineteen (*Smiles nervously.*) and she's, you know, a bit young for her age. She's in bed now. (*He giggles strangely.*) She goes to bed very early . . .

KRAMER: Tucked in safe?

STEPHEN (*smiles oddly to himself*): Yes – tucked in. She had her hair cut yesterday. She looked terrific.

KRAMER (*gently firm*): I don't want any more mistakes Stephen.

He turns. DAVID is standing there. DAVID should be 12½ years old, or as near as is practical. He is small, with very big blue eyes; he is dressed in red velvet trousers, white silk shirt and is wearing a hat. He holds a large cloth bag – like a laundry bag.

(*Taking DAVID in for a split second.*) I'm afraid you've come to the wrong place – this is out of bounds to the public.

DAVID *stands there, grinning.*

STEPHEN: Sir . . .

KRAMER: you can grin as much as you like my friend – this is out of bounds.

STEPHEN (*trying to get his attention*): Sir . . .

KRAMER (*staring at DAVID who remains completely still*): What did I just say?

STEPHEN: Sir that . . .

KRAMER (*cutting him off*): Stephen show this kid down the hill . . .

STEPHEN: But sir . . .

KRAMER *turns away from* DAVID.

KRAMER: His parents – or parent – may have abandoned him.

STEPHEN: Sir – that's Mister David.

KRAMER: Mister (*He turns round.*) Mister David. (*He looks at* DAVID.) What this small kid here . . . ?

STEPHEN: That's right sir.

KRAMER (*slight smile*): And he's not a dwarf?

KRAMER *turns to* CAROLINE.

Is this true?

CAROLINE: Yes of course. Haven't you seen pictures of him . . . ?

STEPHEN: He's a recent success.

KRAMER: They're getting younger and younger, aren't they?

STEPHEN (*slight smile*): The latest wave, sir.

They glance towards DAVID.

He's the one who breaks things just by staring at them, and moves things without touching them . . . amongst other things.

DAVID (*sharp, clear, young voice, London accent*): And who are you?

KRAMER: George Kramer, my apologies. I didn't recognise you.

DAVID: Yes, I saw.

He puts down what he is carrying.

You haven't heard of me then . . .

KRAMER (*watching him very closely*): I think I saw something in the Daily Mail...

DAVID: I've never been in the Daily Mail. (*Slight pause.*) There was a centre page spread in the Sun.

Removes his headgear to reveal his hair which is snow white.

He hasn't heard of me.

He turns and stares at STEPHEN.

It doesn't worry me . . . makes a change.

KRAMER: So you're this new phenomenon are you? I think people have been looking for you.

DAVID (*staring back through his large eyes*): And did they find me . . . ?

He turns and glares towards CAROLINE.

Who's that weird looking girl – is she going to gaol?

CAROLINE (*slight smile*): Not if she can help it.

KRAMER (*lightly, glancing at her*): Can you try to keep quiet until we come back to you.

DAVID (*suddenly sharp*): How high's the stage, I need to know right now.

KRAMER: Radio down, Stephen, and tell them we've found their young star.

DAVID (*very sharp*): I asked you a question, Mr Kramer, a technical question.

KRAMER: And I don't know the answer.

DAVID (*straight at him*): Perhaps you should try to find out.

KRAMER *moves, touches* DAVID's *cloth bag.*

KRAMER: What you got inside here?

DAVID: DON'T TOUCH THAT – it's my equipment.

KRAMER *glances at* STEPHEN, *slight amused smile.*

DAVID, *sharp, staring backwards and forwards.*

Why you grinning . . . Why did you look at him like that?

I'm only going to ask you one more time – *how high* is the stage? How many feet? (*Very sharply.*) And the lights? Have they got brutes rigged up here?

KRAMER: Why don't you go and look. (*Slight dangerous pause.*)

DAVID (*suddenly produces a watch*): I've got a new digital watch. It just stopped, (*Accusingly.*) thought they were never meant to stop.

DAVID *moves slightly.*

I won 40p on the way up here. (*He produces it.*) I told somebody their name.

He is by the table, staring down at his section of it, lifts the cloth and stares underneath.

All this is mine.

He turns from the table.

(*Sharply:*) You can have a boiled sweet – if you like. (*He produces packet, looking pointedly*): It's good for the throat, and bad teeth. Sparkling lemon flavour or wild cherry. Which? come on, you can have some. (*Holds it out.*) Go on, take it, you look as if you need it.

KRAMER: No thank you.

DAVID (*suddenly loud*): I SAID TAKE IT. (*A moment's pause. DAVID lobs whole packet towards KRAMER and turns away.*)

You can't know much, can you?

KRAMER: About what?

DAVID (*dangerous grin*): If you don't know about me they ought to teach you better at the station . . . make you read the papers.

KRAMER (*slight smile, watching him*): Must be bad for your hair, to keep it dyed that colour all the time.

DAVID (*straight at him*): It's not dyed. It grows this colour, doesn't it. It started grey and then went white.
You can get on with what you're doing, you know, don't let me keep you from it. Look at him. (*Lightly, matter of fact:*) He can't take his eyes off, can he.

KRAMER *has moved back to the bag.*

(*Very sharp:*) I said don't touch that – I won't warn you again.

NIGEL *and* LOUISE *enter.*

NIGEL: So there you are, David. (*He smiles.*) We've been looking for you! (*Moves over to greet him.*)

DAVID (*obviously acting*): *Who* are you? (*Turns to KRAMER.*) Who are these people?

NIGEL (*slight smile*): Now David, don't play around.

DAVID (*to* STEPHEN): Do *you* know who they are?

KRAMER (*to* NIGEL): I thought you knew each other.

NIGEL: Of course we do.

DAVID: I've never seen him before in my life, ever. Who is he? I'm not sure he's allowed in this enclosure.

LOUISE (*half whispered to* NIGEL): Is John coming? Perhaps you better wait til he's here, Nigel, he might just be better at it.

NIGEL: Better at what? (*Smiles.*) Don't be stupid.

LOUISE: I mean you must be quite careful. Hasn't he got enormous eyes, like a bush-baby's. Look at all the rings he's wearing.

NIGEL: David, now listen to me carefully.

DAVID (*turns and faces him*): Yes, Mr Richard.

NIGEL (*a smile at this recognition*): Good . . . excellent. Now, where's Mr Duncan, your manager, David, and Mr Cassavetti?

Pause.

DAVID (*faces them, slight smile*): Oh, yes, both my manager and my agent went home. I sent them. They had other engagements. (*Knowing smile.*) They're probably in bed by now.

Sometimes I don't like them watching me, they make me feel uncomfortable.

NIGEL (*astonished, trying to conceal it*): Just say that again – you've sent them home.

DAVID: Yes.

KRAMER: And they went?

DAVID: Of course they went – I wanted them to.

KRAMER (*matter of fact*): Jesus.

DAVID (*suddenly*): I shouldn't think they wanted to be at this crappy concert anyway. (*Glances at* KRAMER.) Why is he looking at me like that? A car is calling for me at midnight. My bodyguard is acting as my legal chaperone tonight. He's 18 stone. Do you want to speak to him? (*He moves to the table.*) I need a drink.

NIGEL (*watching him closely, talking to him very professionally*): Now David, I hope you will understand the situation and show some flexibility. I know we negotiated you would go on at a certain time. And we could stand here throwing clauses at each other, but our main act has been delayed, and I would be very grateful if you could go on as soon as possible, in fact *now*.

Pause. DAVID *looks at him,* NIGEL *faces him in his white suit.*

DAVID: Go on next!

NIGEL: Naturally, you can have a couple of minutes to prepare.

LOUISE: Careful, Nigel.

DAVID (*turns away as if, after all, he hasn't heard* NIGEL's *question*): I've been collecting nuts, small sharp things you get on the ground. (*He produces some.*) I haven't seen them like this before, lying there all over the grass. *Completely free.* Nobody stops you picking them up. There's no charge at all. I've stuffed my pockets, collected seventy-four. Flowers too. (*He produces some flowers, he's pulled out by the roots.*) You can pull them up, nobody minds. You don't have to pay for them either. (*He moves.*) Their heads tear off really easily. This one smells terrible (*He moves.*) I don't know if I like being out in the country.

They watch him for a moment in tense silence.

He looks at NIGEL *and* LOUISE.

Why are you touching each other? You were clutching at him . . . What were you saying . . . ?

LOUISE (*who has been tugging at* NIGEL's *arm; she whispers*): Don't worry – You just have to try again . . .

NIGEL: I'm not worrying.

DAVID: I have to inspect my food now.

He pulls back the cover on the table as they all watch, tense pause, as DAVID *stares at it, his small figure hardly able to stretch across the table.*

It's not right. At all. There is definitely some items missing. But I will overlook it, let you off the hook – for the moment.

They look relieved.

(*Sharp:*) I really only wanted some instant food, but I changed my mind. It would've looked great on this table, wouldn't it?

JOHN *enters.*

LOUISE: John, thank God, you're here – you've got to talk to him.

JOHN (*stares across at* DAVID, *surprised*): Talk to him, to David?

NIGEL: Yes. I think David is beginning to agree to go on next, which will help us all.

DAVID (*suddenly staring at* JOHN): Who's he? I've never seem him before in my life –

JOHN (*familiar manner, they obviously know each other*): David, come on, don't get heavy.

DAVID: Why's he talking to me? I don't know who he is!

JOHN (*carefully*): Someobody's got to go up there – and they're all longing to see you in the flesh – I heard them chattering and whispering about it.

DAVID (*calmly*): Of course. They've paid to see me – not you.

JOHN (*straight back at him*): Absolutely, naturally.

DAVID: I thought your mix sounded really terrible just now.

JOHN: Did you, it was okay.

DAVID: Does your contract specify time of performance? Mine does!

LOUISE: Now listen David, they've all been waiting for you, you know . . .

DAVID: I will have to talk to my manager.

NIGEL (*really sharp*): BUT HE ISN'T HERE.

Slight pause, LOUISE *lifts her camera.*

LOUISE: Look at that. At the slightest sound of a camera – he flicks instantly into a smile.

DAVID (*staring straight at* LOUISE): Because I'm so used to hearing them, aren't I.

Pause, staring straight at them.

IF I go on now . . . I want the first forty rows of people moved back fifty yards.

NIGEL (*astonished*): First forty! Don't be ludicrous, David. It's out of the question.

KRAMER: You can't start moving people now, you'll cause chaos.

DAVID (*his manner brisk, professional*): It's got to be done. I've got to have the right spatial relation . . . I've never performed out of doors before.

Looks between KRAMER *and* NIGEL.

NIGEL: All right, David, I will give orders, we'll try our best.

DAVID: You nodded at each other. I saw – I saw that look (*As* NIGEL *looks at* KRAMER:) Those lights up there! How many watts are those?

NIGEL (*tinge of exasperation*): I haven't the slightest idea, I'm afraid.

DAVID: I need 4,000 watts on stage . . . I must have them.

JOHN: You're fine up there, Dave, no problem, you can see too much . . .

DAVID: And I don't want any of those lightweight video cameras roving around up there, pushing into your face.

NIGEL: I'll move them back, I'll see to it.

DAVID: And there is a slope on the stage, it's got to go.

NIGEL: A slope! David – the stage is *there,* for better or worse, there's nothing we can do now.

DAVID: There is a big slope and its got to go.

Silence, LOUISE *squeezes* NIGEL's *hand.*

You're grabbing at each other again, see, they're doing it again.

NIGEL (*voice sharp*): David! We're in the middle of the bloody country – don't you realise – we can't start making structural alterations now . . . I have built the best stage possible.

DAVID: With a slope. I told you, it's got to go!

KRAMER (*nods at* NIGEL, *looks between them*): We'll see what my boys can do – we may be able to *crank* it.

Pause.

DAVID (*half convinced, he looks from* NIGEL *to* KRAMER): They better do it right.

LOUISE: Yes – they'll crank it for you.

NIGEL (*sharp*): Sssh . . . *Now,* David will you . . .

DAVID (*sudden excited grin*): Can I see the inside of the police car . . . ?

KRAMER (*quick*): When you've done your act you can.

DAVID: But I want to see inside *now.*

NIGEL: All right, quickly David – go on; just have a very quick look . . . ?

KRAMER (*reluctantly*): Stephen – show the kid the car for twenty seconds –

DAVID (*moving towards it with* STEPHEN): Does it have electric windows? (*Pause. He looks back over his shoulder.*) And they must be totally quiet for ten minutes before I start.

He is upstage now with STEPHEN – *peering through the window of the police car.*

LOUISE (*lowering her voice, urgent*): What else will he want? You mustn't let him destroy things . . .

JOHN: He'll do it for now. I could see him tensing ready for it.

NIGEL (*sharp*): We better speak in French as a precaution. Just in case, je crois il est tres fatigué et –

LOUISE: Je crois qu'il est un petit emmerdeur et il n'y a pas de limite a ce qu'il pourrait demander. Alors, il est capable de nous demander de nous déshabiller. Je me demande comment sa mère sait se débattre avec lui. Sans doubt l'a – t – il y a longtemps.

NIGEL: Sa mère n'entre pas en question, l'important est de rester tranquille . . . (*French runs out. Slight tense smile.*) of course now every word of French has suddenly drained away . . .

LOUISE: It's so extraordinary having to be cautious in front of *him.*

KRAMER: Your time is up. You better get ready.

DAVID *turns.*

DAVID: I've got to *sit* inside the car now.

KRAMER: No, that's all you're getting – you can do that afterwards, when you've earned it . . .

DAVID (*steely*): I would like to sit in the car now.

KRAMER: But you can't.

They face each other.

DAVID: I HAVE TO SIT IN THE CAR – before I do it.

KRAMER: You're having a wonderful time aren't you – just playing around . . .

DAVID (*moves downstage slightly*): What did he say? (*He stares at the others.*) What did the man say?

KRAMER: Isn't that right? Get up there and do it now – and stop letting people down, or I'll have you frogmarched up there to do it.

DAVID (*very very quiet*): Did you hear what he said?

Then he screams.

DON'T YOU UNDERSTAND – I'VE GOT TO BE IN THE MOOD. (*He continues to shout.*) You fucking idiot. You're not allowed to say things like that to me for fucks sake. I'm the only one who does it, WHO HAS TO DO IT, and I have to be in the mood. You think it's easy – what I do (*He screams.*) it's the most difficult thing in the world.

He starts hurling bottles across the stage at the police car with extraordinary violence, they hit its side.

It's more difficult than anything you can do you bloody idiot. You're such a bloody stupid fucking idiot.

He throws a bottle at the car.

I want to kill you. *I'm not going on now – never again, and nothing you can do can make me.*

NIGEL: David!

He goes. They all look at KRAMER.

KRAMER (*sharp*): Somebody go after him.

LOUISE (*moving to the exit, urgent*): That's really done it, hasn't it! We'll never ever get him back now. (*To* KRAMER:) Why did you have to say that?

She goes.

NIGEL (*calls after her*): Louise . . .

KRAMER: Stephen! Go and help the lady catch up with him!

STEPHEN *glances at* CAROLINE. STEPHEN *goes.*

NIGEL (*turning straight at* KRAMER *very acid and hostile*): You really shouldn't have done that you know. You do seem to have astonishing talent for interference. I now appear to have no light show, no Mister David and we go into overtime in 9½ minutes.

KRAMER: He had to be stopped. He would have gone on making conditions for days.

NIGEL: You're absolutely wrong of course. He was about to agree. Now I will have to do something I profoundly disapprove of – I will have to go on myself and make a speech.

KRAMER: Go on yourself?

NIGEL: I'll have to hold things together personally – till they arrive. (*To* JOHN:) and you're coming with me.

JOHN (*surprised*): Me. Am I? I'll stand next to you if you like – if I really have to.

He immediately pours himself another tomato juice.

I can't imagine anything I want to do less than go up there again.

NIGEL (*sharp*): Where's my radio?

JOHN (*wandering up*): My first festival thirteen years ago. Thirteen. I was bowled over to get up for a minute spot on stage. I told everyone about it, even my mother. When I'm up there now I feel I can walk out across their faces.

NIGEL (*staring down at his white suit, there is a slight stain on this, he rubs it. To* JOHN): I am of course taking a bit of a gamble with tonight, there's no denying it. But I wanted to create a feeling of celebration, give them something to revel in, especially during such grey times; I'm just adding a splash of colour. There are simpler ways of making money of course, although I'm still going to make a profit out of tonight. Very few people know how to spend their money imaginatively now. How to give people what they want. But they're going to get it tonight.

KRAMER (*glancing out*): People are meeting each other for the first and last time. Beginning to touch each other in the dark. A lot of them have walked from Southampton, others may have stolen cars from London to reach here, some even will have robbed old ladies; God knows why – they must be hoping for something.

NIGEL *looks at* KRAMER.

NIGEL: You know nothing about it . . . (*To* JOHN:) Right.

KRAMER (*firm*): Don't apologise when you're up there.

NIGEL (*sharp, steely smile*): Thank you, yes.

KRAMER (*calm*): I'm telling you not to apologise. And don't give exact times. Just look them in the eyes – pick one spot and stare straight at it.

NIGEL (*fast, loud*): Yes! O.K. Yes!

KRAMER: Keep it short, sharp, and confident . . . don't hesitate.

NIGEL (*loud*): Please, just refrain . . .

He crosses over to the table.

KRAMER (*very slight grin*): And pray for help.

NIGEL (*back to* KRAMER, *at the table, hardly concentrating*): So you're a religious man are you? A churchgoer?

KRAMER: Occasionally. (*He smiles to himself.*) I ring up beforehand and see what hymn is showing.

STEPHEN *enters.*

KRAMER (*sharp*): No sign of him?

STEPHEN: No sir, that's right. The little bugger's completely vanished . . .

JOHN (*sudden sharp*): I'm sweating and leaking all over. Come on! Let's get it over with.

NIGEL: Certainly.

They move to go.

KRAMER (*after him*): Remember to keep completely still when you stand up there.

NIGEL (*very sharp*): Could you *just stop giving me advice*, I don't know what you're trying to do but I wish you'd stop it. And if you have to come down too please keep totally out of the way. They might start throwing things if you're around.

They go.

KRAMER (*to* CAROLINE): Don't worry

we'll be with you shortly.

CAROLINE (*staring back*): You don't have to apologise.

KRAMER: And I wasn't.

CAROLINE (*holding up the clean white handkerchief*): Do you want this back?

KRAMER: You can keep it, as a souvenir.

CAROLINE: Really? Can I have it autographed then!

KRAMER: Not just now.

CAROLINE (*slight smile*): You thought I was serious.

KRAMER: Only half.

He moves to go, then turns, looks at her.

I do get asked for my autograph occasionally, by new young, policemen and trainee traffic wardens.

LOUISE (*goes running and calling*): Nigel, Nigel.

She stops as she sees KRAMER. *They stare at each other for a moment.*

You're still here.

KRAMER: I was just about to go and watch your husband. He's going to make an announcement on stage.

Very slight pause between them.

LOUISE (*sharply*): Go on then.

KRAMER *goes.*

As we hear the noise of clapping and whistling, LOUISE *stands smoking nervously, some distance from* STEPHEN *and* CAROLINE.

CAROLINE *turns, her manner is pre-occupied. She looks at* STEPHEN.

He must give you a hard time.

STEPHEN: No, madam, he doesn't.

LOUISE (*moving, her thoughts leaping from one thing to another*): I am not sure this is the wisest move Nigel has ever made to go down there. (*She smacks at her arm.*) I am getting bitten all over now. The mosquitoes seem to be the size of dragonflies in this part of the world, come whirring towards one like small aircraft. (*Looks at* STEPHEN *and* CAROLINE.) Don't they? (*She moves again without waiting for them to reply.*) Of course he may do it splendidly.

CAROLINE (*suddenly*): You should go and take some pictures.

LOUISE *looks up, surprised at her intervention.*

LOUISE: Maybe, it's only a hobby this, of course, so many people take good photos now anyway. I dabble, I take photographs of my husband's projects, his various schemes.

CAROLINE: Ah!

LOUISE (*glaring at* CAROLINE *and then moves away*): You can feel the chilly stare and disapproval. A real icy blast. (*She looks at* CAROLINE.) Have you done something very serious – to get arrested?

CAROLINE: I'm not arrested. I haven't done anything as it happens.

LOUISE: Really (*She stares at her.*) I thought you had. (*She moves away.*) I hate it when things don't go according to plan. My insides are wobbling. (*Tugging at her cigarette.*) I don't really want to see this. I'm going to stay up here, and half close my eyes.

The noise of restless clapping and whistling becomes louder as home-made wooden stage and scaffolding rolls in front of the permanent set. It is quite high though it doesn't have to be broad. It has a microphone on a stand on it – and a back to it covered in some bright emblem from whose side people can enter. As it rolls on we hear a flat electrician's voice over the tannoy, penetrating through the noise of whistles and cat calls saying 'testing . . . testing . . . testing . . . one two buckle my shoe . . . ' etc. Then very briskly a burst of music, a spotlight hits an empty stage, and JOHN *walks into it. Applause breaks out. His manner is totally changed – to that of a performer.*

JOHN: Yes – I'm working overtime today, God knows why. Certainly not because of you lot. You're not going to get any more of me anyway – but we've got a word from our sponsor for you, how can you resist it? So just give him a good hearing – because it's not his fault – and he's going to try to explain himself.

NIGEL *comes on.*

NIGEL (*his sharp dry voice ringing out through the microphone*): Good evening. It is nice to see you all. *Now* – it is quite clear that you haven't paid to see me (*Sharp smile.*) apart from anything else I was thrown out of the school choir, for selling cannabis to the choristers.

No response, he smiles tensely.

So I'll make this very brief. (*He glances down.*) I'm treading carefully because I'm told some parts of the stage are dangerous. (*He smiles.*) I'm aware – as you are aware – we haven't been following the published programme. And this is because there have been some mild and rather irritating technical hitches.

A few people start to slow handclap.

I know what it feels like to be kept waiting, especially if you have paid your money. It's intensely annoying I know – (*Sharp nervous smile.*) and when it's happened to me I've wanted to tear those responsible apart – being one of the least patient people on earth.

Slow handclap is beginning to grow.

But I can assure you that I'm doing everything in my power to get 'normal service resumed as soon as possible'. I have hired the best technicians in England for tonight – the most successful artistes and as you can see some of the best weather.

Slow handclapping really intensifying – it is extremely loud.

NIGEL (*standing in his white suit in the middle of the stage*): Now come on – we don't need any of that.

But slow handclap just increases.

I can *guarantee* you that we'll have things happening up here you will never have seen before . . .

Slow handclap really loud and steady.

Now give one a chance – this is not really needed. As well as being rather stupid – will you just be quiet for a moment. (*He is hardly audible for a moment.*)

Will you just SHUT UP a minute – Will you just BE QUIET while I tell you . . . (*Loud.*) COULD YOU JUST . . .

Very loud slow handclap, he cannot make himself heard. NIGEL *stares out – only just able to contain his fury, he walks off the stage – there's a very slight pause, bare stage, with the deafening slow handclap. Then* KRAMER *walks onto the stage and up to the microphone. The noise increases even further.*

KRAMER: All right. Shall we have some quiet. Some quiet.

He stands there, the noise drops slightly for a moment.

The concert . . . the programme of the concert tonight is not my concern (*Slight smile.*) that is not my job. I just want to make it understood (*He grins.*) in no uncertain terms, that we're all in this bloody field together, and we're going to get through this night in *one piece.* (*Looking straight.*) and that includes you . . .

The slow handclap is really loud again.

I hope we're all going to be sensible . . . it would make a change.

KRAMER *stands very still for a moment as the slow handclap continues, then he leaves the stage. Music immediately starts coming over the speakers mingling with the slow handclap as the houselights come up slowly.*

ACT TWO

Night. It is after midnight. A picnic. White sheets spread over the grass centre stage. The cyclorama is black, the arc lights are shining down on the scene brightly.
The police car's lights are on, shining into the wings, and its doors are open. JOHN *is leaning against the bonnet smoking a long thin cigar.*
KEN *is sitting on the white sheet down stage, drinking a can of beer.*
LOUISE *and* NIGEL *are sitting near each other on the garden chairs.*
STEPHEN *is standing behind* CAROLINE *who is sitting on the very edge of the white sheet, upstage, occasionally glancing at a book beside her.*
The table is standing uncovered. The food and drink shining under the coloured lights that run along the awning. The food and drink is totally untouched.
NIGEL *is sipping champagne – there are a stack of champagne bottles apart from the main table by the tea urns.*

NIGEL (*into his walkie-talkie*): So I should

hope. (*Sharp.*) Not before time! Keep the photographers in the wrong place. Yes . . . Good.

NIGEL (*he clicks off the radio*): The main act's car's been sighted coming up the hill. They're arriving. He's going to let me know as soon as they are here.

LOUISE: Thank God for that.

NIGEL (*smiles*): Good news.

JOHN (*leaning against the bonnet blowing smoke rings*): You reckon do you?

NIGEL *moving around with a bottle of champagne.*

NIGEL (*to* KEN): Drink?

KEN: I shouldn't – but I'm going to.

KEN *seems very preoccupied – he takes an immediate gulp of champagne.*

NIGEL (*gently to* LOUISE): Why don't you drink something. You haven't eaten or drunk all day.

LOUISE (*smoking*): I'm fine. I just don't want anything.

NIGEL (*right by her*): And you must stop chain smoking, it's one of the ugliest sights in the world. I really hate it.

LOUISE (*slight smile*): Perhaps you should try not to look. I haven't smoked this much since boarding school. We used to go up to the Biology Lab, among the jelly fish, and hang our heads out of the window and long to be eighteen. (*She turns away.*)

JOHN (*staring towards* CAROLINE): Is he, do you think, going to put that girl in the boot of his car?

KEN: I don't know what she's doing still here. He says he doesn't want to over-crowd the farm location. But it's an extra-ordinary thing to do – totally irregular.

LOUISE (*to* JOHN): Why *you* still with us John?

JOHN: I don't seem to be able to tear myself away. I can never sleep on nights like this.

NIGEL (*standing, sipping champagne*): Although I hate to admit it, your boss's stage appearance appears to have worked. So far! Between us we stopped them going berserk.

LOUISE (*smiling to herself*): Yes you did – didn't you.

NIGEL: Despite it being a rather odd thing for him to do. Perhaps I should have hired him to organise the whole night! (*He smiles to himself.*)

KEN (*who has begun to eat a battered sandwich out of his pocket*): He organised a policeman's funeral last year. He'd only been a chief constable a few months. It was a winter funeral. He planned the whole thing with incredible detail, placed the mourners in long lines in the snow, had harsh trumpets and black carpets, all timed just as daylight was fading. It was like a film.

NIGEL: He's very religious. He confessed to me – he goes to church.

KEN: He approved a new cut of the uniform which is his right. A tailored jacket with a new stylish centre vent.

LOUISE: Really! I thought you all look alike.

KEN (*biting into the sandwich, deeply absorbed*): He's always been a highflier. Mind you, when I first met him, and I knew him as a constable, I remember thinking he's young enough to be my son, . . . far too many of them, but also over-sensitive, a real touchy character, couldn't *handle any of the rougher stuff at all. Any violence made him ill.* Very good at paper work he was. (*He wipes his mouth with a handkerchief, continues fast loud with feeling:*) And then when we were both in the Met he had a funny time then . . . he felt it was corrupt and inefficient.

JOHN (*blowing smoke*): So policemen are corrupt . . . I would never have guessed.

KEN (*turns, stares at JOHN*): They're rotten apples everywhere – even here!

He takes a large gulp of wine.

He was completely clean, made a shining point of it. He felt he wasn't being appreciated, wasn't clambering up the ladder fast enough. He nearly left the force.

Another gulp of wine.

He wasn't married then – in those days I never saw him within a hundred yards of a girl. He went and lived in Willesden for

three years, in this bare little room, just one gas ring on the landing. He used to live off raw onions and grapefruit and he kept white mice like a schoolboy and wrote poems. Never went out except to work. He wants to be the youngest police commissioner ever – (*Drinks.*) but he does make mistakes you see. Plenty of senior officers in the county want to see him fall flat on the pavement – especially the A.C.C.'s they want him out! Want him to make a *real* mistake. (*With feeling:*) I've never thought him a good policeman.

Very slight pause; LOUISE looks straight at KEN.

LOUISE (*pointed*): I didn't know policemen were jealous of each other.

She lights another cigarette with the top of her old one.

NIGEL: *Please* stop doing that Louise – you must have smoked more than seventy already tonight. Why won't you eat something, *come on!*

He pushes one of KEN's sandwiches up to her mouth.

LOUISE: No, Nigel, I don't want it.

NIGEL: I don't know what's the matter with you tonight. (*By her:*) Come on – you'll fade into nothing.

KRAMER *is standing there.*

NIGEL (*looks up from by LOUISE*): It's you . . .

KRAMER (*grinning*): I just been for a walk, look the place over.

NIGEL: Things are under control again. Their car, believe it or not, has been sighted. We can even forget about Mister David.

Alarm clock goes off, loud ringing, they all look round. NIGEL stands up.

NIGEL: It's all right – (*The ringing continues loud.*) That is me. (*He takes the clock out of his pocket – it continues to ring.*) And that means as everyone will have guessed – we are now in golden time!

Bell ringing.

LOUISE: Can't you switch it off.

NIGEL (*fiddling with the clock – the ring continues*): It's got quite a vicious ring hasn't it.

LOUISE: It is stoppable, isn't it?

NIGEL: Just shut up. Come on stop, just shut up. It means I'm paying an extra thousand pounds every twenty five minutes.

KRAMER: Twenty-five minutes!

NIGEL (*suddenly quite edgy*): Yes! I haven't the faintest idea why it's twenty-five minutes – but it is!

The ringing stops.

KRAMER (*glancing round – he hasn't been offered a drink*): Get us a drink Stephen. (*Grins.*) You're eating too much Ken, as usual, have to crawl off this patch on all fours, your stomach scraping the ground.

KEN (*sharp, back at him*): I don't think so George, I feel even more alert than when I started tonight.

JOHN (*suddenly*): You've been mingling with the audience have you – *all by yourself.*

KRAMER (*moving around the white sheet, further downstage*): Yes – I've just walked in among them.

KEN: Among them.

KRAMER: They didn't get a chance to recognise me. They won't give us any more trouble now.

NIGEL: And they'll get their reward in a minute.

KRAMER (*suddenly loud*): We've seen it all before Ken haven't we. As young constables way back, walking along to meet the Rockers as they were tearing up deckchairs beside the Serpentine. They soon quietened down. (*He smiles.*) Youngsters are all the same!

KEN: I don't think I remember that – the Serpentine?

KRAMER (*sharp, fast, smiling*): You must have been in one of those decaying little offices . . . then of course shepherding the ban the bomb marches all that way, when a few brave youngsters were beginning to wear American jeans for the first time, very clean and smart, and holding hands rather shyly while sheltering in doorways during a thunderstorm.

KEN: Yes it always seemed to be raining on those walks, didn't it?

KRAMER: A few homosexuals showing themselves in public, touching each other cautiously when they thought no-one was watching – half expecting to be hit. It was just a social occasion for all of them, they needed to be in a group, they knew they couldn't change a thing . . .

LOUISE *watching him closely.*

KEN: They were very calm really. (*With feeling:*) It was just such a bloody long walk!

KRAMER (*carrying on, smiling*): Then the Vietnam marches in the sixties, just the same, a social occasion, they came for some lively fun. But beginning to get more violent now. With those it always seemed to be very hot didn't it, burning inside your uniform, as they screamed at you. And people's bare feet treading accidentally on broken glass in the streets, and I had to get out my own sticky-plaster and patch up this kid's foot, his big toe, right there on the pavement. He'd been trying to maim me a moment earlier.

KEN: You shouldn't have done that – against regulations.

KRAMER (*swings round*): She was probably there.

CAROLINE (*looking up*): Do you mean me? You're wrong. I wasn't.

KRAMER: Yes, I think so, somewhere in that mass of headbands and long hair. There's probably a photograph of you deep down somewhere. (*He smiles.*) We're coming for you straight after this picnic. (*Turns, smiles.*) And what have they got now? – like this lot tonight. Still doing it in the long grass of course. I just passed two people making love amongst the fir cones, must be rather damp by now, clinging to each other like they were going to fall. They were really very young, at that age I wouldn't have known what end was the right end.

LOUISE (*suddenly, tugging at her cigarette*): I don't know where they find the energy to do it so much – I mean we must do it about once a fortnight I suppose.

NIGEL (*truly startled*): Louise? . . . (*Trying to remain cool.*) I expect it's about that.

LOUISE: That's not such a secret is it? (*She smiles.*) People look at me and think she's very good-looking or quite good-looking, they've seen me at film premiers, looking furiously exotic, all done up in cellophane and drawing pins, wearing the latest hideous clothes, and they think she must have such a whirlwind, such a hectic sex life.

NIGEL (*by her, out of the corner of his mouth*): Louise . . .

LOUISE: In fact, it's a perfectly reasonable one. (*Smiles.*) I just wish people didn't talk about it so much, endlessly (*To KRAMER:*) don't you?

KRAMER: I never listen.

NIGEL: Louise, I think that may be enough.

LOUISE: You're made to believe you should be doing it all the time, even in your sleep.

JOHN (*blowing smoke in the air*): But they do don't they, kids now, even at meal times. I see them locked into each other in the queues for my concerts.

KEN: Young girls especially, it's the young girls.

LOUISE (*smiling, smoking*): I find myself sitting in front of the tele staring obsessively at weather forecasters and cabinet ministers wondering how much they have (*Glancing at KRAMER.*) childish isn't it . . .

KRAMER *watching her.*

NIGEL (*trying to remain composed*): Louise I think it may be time for a walk.

LOUISE: . . . and then something violent comes up on the screen, the nightly dose of smashed bodies, and I sit there in front of it like a piece of frozen yoghurt, unable to look, and unable to switch it off. (*She smiles.*) I'm often alone in the flat staring at the phone, thinking it'd be funny if you could dial an orgasm like dialling the recipe of the day. It'll be the latest thing. Use the receiver as a . . .

NIGEL: I think you've entertained us enough Louise, (*Whispers:*) Love could you just . . .

LOUISE (*carrying on*): I really *wish* people would stop trying to make one feel inadequate.

NIGEL: Nobody's listening to this.

JOHN: That is patently untrue!

LOUISE (*smiling*): When I was about thirteen a man with a glass eye flashed at me in Kensington Gardens.

NIGEL: Louise please! You're in front of the police. (*Trying to smile.*) I hardly think this is suitable conversation.

LOUISE (*carrying on*): I didn't mind. I was quite curious. He had green pants. It was under the big avenue of plane trees. (*To KRAMER:*) They've cut them down now. He said would I have sex with him in his flat in St. Albans. After a little thought I declined.

NIGEL (*by her*): Louise, *please stop this.*

LOUISE: He said – I'll never forget it, he said I really pity you growing up now in all this and he started to cry, he cried so much.

JOHN (*loud*): His glass eye fell out!

LOUISE (*very quiet*): I now know what he meant of course.

NIGEL: This is all total fiction. (*Trying to smile.*) She's made all this up.

JOHN (*giggles to himself*): I wonder if we'll ever feel nostalgic about this year – the most enjoyable petrol queues we've sat in.

KRAMER (*sharp to STEPHEN*): Come on Kid – where's that drink, we need it!

STEPHEN (*who's struggling with a corkscrew; the cork has got stuck*): I'm doing it sir, it's very stiff – won't be a moment.

LOUISE (*carrying on*): And when I was fifteen years old . . .

Somebody screams 'SHUT UP' from a long distance away, but perfectly audible. LOUISE *looks round, totally startled.*

What on earth was that?

KRAMER: Somebody shouting about the noise of the taped music from the houses over there.

NIGEL: No need to remind me it's only a tape.

Noise from the walkie-talkie murmuring.

KRAMER (*smiles*): People often come rushing out to me when we're driving around at night, they stand in front of the car, sometimes dressed only in their pyjamas, asking me to make the noise less, the late night parties, screaming motor-cycles. (*He smiles.*) I've tried to make Southampton a quieter place.

Radio noise really buzzing.

NIGEL (*clicks on the radio, urbane smile*): Yes, Simon, glad to hear from you. (*His voice changes.*) I see . . . I heard yes (*Pause.*) I'll come back to you in a minute Simon.

He looks up expressionless.

KRAMER: What's happened?

NIGEL: Their car's arrived now.

LOUISE: Oh good.

NIGEL: But there's just a very slight problem – they're not inside it.

KRAMER: What?

LOUISE: Don't be ridiculous. What do you mean?

NIGEL: No, I mean it. They aren't inside.

LOUISE: Have they looked properly?

JOHN (*smiles at them all*): Maybe they're hiding in the ashtrays.

NIGEL (*his voice quiet*): The chauffeur says they'll be along in an hour. Definitely. (*He suddenly moves abruptly.*) Christ, this is beginning to look just a little nasty.

He stares at the table of untouched food.

LOUISE: Try to sit down, it may be better if you try to keep still.

KRAMER (*to* STEPHEN): See they check the car – make sure it's not a hoax.

NIGEL (*moving*): When they arrive – I feel it is quite likely I will do them rather a violent injury. I mean what on earth do they think they're doing. You realise the poor buggers out there have paid £8 for a ticket!

STEPHEN *is on radio.*

KRAMER: We're checking the car.

LOUISE: Just try to keep terribly still.

NIGEL (*trying to sit still, straight at* KRAMER): You realise of course *you* going up there will have keyed them up – made them much more over-excited.

KRAMER: You don't have to worry. It's

all handleable (*Sharp to* STEPHEN:) come on kid we've been waiting for that drink for too long.

NIGEL (*wiping his face, sitting*): Yes, I need one.

KRAMER (*to* STEPHEN): What's the matter with you?

STEPHEN (*who is struggling with the cork still not out*): I know sir I'll (*He really pulls at it, straining, everybody watching him.*)

KRAMER: Come on Stephen – it's only a bottle!

STEPHEN (*suddenly throws the bottle down on the ground*): The bloody thing won't come sir! I can't do it.

KEN (*furious, shocked at this*): For Chrissake lad – what do you think you're doing . . . ?

KRAMER (*steely*): Pick it up at once, Stephen, go on.

STEPHEN (*ashamed*): I'm sorry sir – I got frustrated.

STEPHEN *moves to another bottle.* NIGEL *who has been sitting terribly still, suddenly jumps up.*

NIGEL: It's just beginning to really hit me – (*His voice rising:*) Christ – this is like one of those vicious, really mean nightmares – where you're giving a party for hundreds of people . . .

JOHN: Thousands in this case.

NIGEL: And they all turn up, and suddenly you find there's no food or drink in the house at all, NONE. And you're constantly smiling and watching the kitchen door, but you know they're going to realise any moment – I mean they're not THAT STUPID – and then what will they do? (*He glances at* KRAMER.) One must not panic, we've still got Mister David somewhere. (*He looks at* JOHN, *very sharp.*) You could help.

JOHN (*quiet*): I don't think so.

NIGEL: Sitting there like a vulture or whatever I wish you'd leave us.

KEN's *walkie-talkie is buzzing;* KRAMER *picks it up from the floor.*

KRAMER (*sharp*): O.K. Yes, right. When? Where? We'll be over right away.

LOUISE (*looks up*): What's happened?

NIGEL *looks up.*

KRAMER: There's been a slight incident . . . a youngster has been stabbed.

Shocked pause. They all look at him.

LOUISE (*truly startled*): What?

NIGEL (*very shaken, quiet*): Oh Christ . . . I just knew it . . .

KEN (*to* KRAMER): Where?

KRAMER: They've just found him, under the trees, down by the toilets. Don't worry – he's not dead, yet.

NIGEL (*sitting frozen to his chair, voice very quiet*): This is the beginning, it really is.

KRAMER: Stephen, here. Clear the mess up. (*He indicates the picnic mess to be cleared, then switches onto* KEN's *walkie-talkie very animated and sharp:*) O.K. I want double the men on the gates, no, don't touch the men round the stage.

KEN (*getting up*): What, north or south toilets?

KRAMER: North. (*Into the walkie-talkie fast:*) Well *find some.* (*Slight grin into the radio glancing at* STEPHEN.) I've got one spare one up here for a start, who I could easily part with. Have they moved the kid? . . . Fine . . . I want *no sirens,* absolute quiet, IF I hear a siren the man responsible will spend the rest of his short life indoors. Superintendent Daniels will come down to join you . . .

JOHN (*still leaning against car*): I think this may be the point where I take my leave.

He doesn't move.

KRAMER (*to* KEN): We'll go down one at a time. I don't want the whole spot crawling with men and vehicles. You go first, I'll be with you when I've finished here. (KEN *moving slowly. Sharp:*) Come on Ken – you can finish that later!

KEN (*putting his sandwiches away, resentful*): I've finished already George.

He goes.

KRAMER (*flicking instantaneously back onto the radio*): And I want the chopper – wherever it is . . . That is beside the point.

NIGEL: We've got to stay calm somehow.

LOUISE (*moving, chewing the end of her hair*): I think I want to go home . . .

NIGEL: Don't move Louise. (*Hanging onto her.*) You're staying right here.

KRAMER (*swings round looks at them*): There's nothing unusual in this happening – in Madison Gardens they can't have a fifty year old ex-hairdresser in a toupé singing his golden favourites without at least seven people getting sliced to pieces. (*Into the walkie-talkie.*) OK – and make sure there's never less than three. Yes, – which hospital? I'll call there on my way back – and see him myself.

JOHN (*moving from the car*): When things get uncomfortable – there's only one thing to do.

He moves to go.

Have a nice party . . . ?

KRAMER (*turns sharply*): No – you stay here.

JOHN *stops and stands completely still.*

LOUISE: I'm not staying here, there's going to be a riot. (*She gets up and pulls away.*) What are we doing in this bloody field anyway. I should be in bed by now.

NIGEL: Louise (*Holds onto her hand.*) you're staying here . . .

LOUISE: Let go. (*Sharp.*) Let go of me Nigel. (*She pulls away crosses upstage to the exit then turns. Straight to* KRAMER:) I hope you'll try to do something. I don't think my husband can manage this anymore. It seems to be slipping away from him. You'll have to do your best. (*Sharp.*) Won't you?

She goes.

NIGEL (*after her*): Louise . . . wait . . . (*He turns and faces* KRAMER *really loud:*) You know THIS IS IT. DON'T YOU? This is *really* it. (*His voice rising to a shout:*) I mean what happens if they start fighting now, I thought you were meant to be able to handle crowds. (*Almost screaming:*) For Chrissake everything's gone wrong since you arrived – every-thing. (*Waving his arm.*) This is about the worst thing that can happen now, you realise, the really worst – and its happened. (*He moves, his tone just slightly calmer, really steely.*) You really better be able to do something or I warn you . . . (*He moves to go.*) I *warn you,* I really mean that.

KRAMER: You don't have to worry.

NIGEL: Worry. (*He screams:*) Worry – that is a totally idiotic thing to say.

NIGEL *goes.* KRAMER *turns to* JOHN.

JOHN: You wanted to say something?

KRAMER: Yes. I think you could go on again don't you.

JOHN: I don't quite understand.

KRAMER: Sing again. I'm asking you to . . .

JOHN (*straight back at him*): I'm afraid not – I'm too stiff.

KRAMER (*startled*): Too stiff? You were only up there half an hour.

JOHN (*tone changes*): Sorry mate – I can't face it. (*Sudden genuine smile.*) I really can't. I feel bruised all over after the last one. I can hardly move . . .

He moves with difficulty – like in the first act – KRAMER *watches uncertain if he's joking or not.*

KRAMER: Bruised? But nobody did anything to you.

JOHN (*looks at him*): Touch me – and it hurts. It really does.

JOHN *touches his own arm and winces.*

Like I've been kicked down some stone steps. I'm not kidding now, I can hardly sit down. (*He smiles.*) I can't explain it any better, and there's nothing I can do about it – silly isn't it. I'll be throwing it in I expect, when I've paid for my new home in Weybridge. Eleven bedrooms! (*He moves to go.*) Sorry about that I'd like to have helped Mr Kramer, and you need some help, but you see I can't. At least things can't get any worse. (*Slight smile.*) Can they?

He goes.

KRAMER (*watching him go*): Scattering like pigeons. (*He turns.*) I think I'll have something to drink Stephen. Quick. (*As he moves.*) Clear this mess up too. (*He indicates some of the picnic mess. To* CAROLINE:) Could you move back a little.

CAROLINE (*surprised*): Back?

KRAMER: Yes. A little.

She moves away from him upstage.

Like that – a little further, I'll tell you when to stop . . . (*He grins.*) I was always bad at point duty . . . There. Stop!

CAROLINE *is upstage, away from him he stares at her across the breadth of the stage.*

It's a pity about this . . .

CAROLINE (*cutting him off, slight smile*): Because you were just getting round to me?

KRAMER: Yes, that's right. Now of course I have no men free to move you.

CAROLINE (*smiles*): You could always let me go.

KRAMER: I could – but I'm not going to, yet.

He turns away, his back to her.

Don't worry.

He starts pacing in the space he has cleared, his adrenalin really flowing. Sharp orders into the walkie-talkie, very fast.

Everybody who leaves the compound from now on is to be stopped and searched. Yes! Outside the perimeter, a good fifty yards Superintendant Daniels' gone down there . . . is that firmly understood?

He listens for a second.

I know! But we haven't got *anybody to go on stage* at the moment . . . Obviously! . . . But we're not going to let that happen – are we?

STEPHEN *moving towards him with a bottle.*

STEPHEN: Is there anything I can do sir – to help?

A piercing shout comes from far away in the distance, KRAMER's *head turns. During the scene catcalls and then spattered barracking handclap starts in the distance, gradually growing in intensity.*

KRAMER (*looks back*): Just open that and make a job of it this time . . .

STEPHEN (*careful, holding the champagne bottle, his hand shaking, he pulls the cork*

top off. He laughs nervously): Good start
... Yes ... sorry about just now sir – the
bottle.

He is terribly tense, nervous giggles.

KRAMER: What on earth's happening to
you tonight?

STEPHEN (*giggles*): Yes sir I ...

KRAMER (*sharp into the walkie-talkie*):
And keep it like that – absolutely fixed.
I'm not interested, you'll just have to
manage it. *Now,* get me the compère,
whatever his name.

Turns, glances very quickly at
CAROLINE *who is reading her book.*

Don't run away, we haven't forgotten
you. (*To* STEPHEN *sharp:*) What is it
Stephen?

STEPHEN (*nervously, still holding the
champagne bottle*): It seems an extraordinary time to tell you sir – I can't really
do it, when you're in the middle ...

KRAMER (*cutting him off*): I want you to
tell me now. (*Slight smile.*) I'm good at
doing several different things at once –
you may have noticed ...

STEPHEN (*bracing himself*): It's ... it's ...

KRAMER (*into the walkie-talkie*): OK
thanks (*Turns.*) It's about your wife?

STEPHEN: Yes, you see sir, she's really
young and excitable, and ...

KRAMER: And she's got another bloke?

STEPHEN's *face whips round.*

STEPHEN: You guessed!

He glances in admiration.

It's a good guess.

KRAMER: Yes. (*Glancing over towards*
CAROLINE.) I can move her if you like
(*Louder:*) but she's not listening ...

STEPHEN (*grins nervously*): No no ...

KRAMER (*very fast into the radio*): He's
the one that's been making those idiotic
speeches. No! – Yes that one. Get him on
the end of a radio quickly. I need to talk
to him.

Almost without a break he turns back to
STEPHEN.

Yes Stephen?

STEPHEN (*very very nervous and pent up
giggles – fast, holding the bottle with the
corkscrew in the cork*): And you see it's – I
don't know how to put this – it's so stupid
(*Broad grin.*) but you see it's about this
time she's with him, you know, I mean,
they'll be at it now sir, you can't really
HELP having the picture in your mind,
it's really clear tonight in fact, him coming
into the room, and going to draw the
curtains, and you see ... (*Loud giggle.*)
It's really stupid ... each time I push this
in for instance – (*His hand tightens on the
corkscrew.*) I know it's like a schoolkid – I
push it in and it just comes into my mind,
this picture of them together, having
intercourse sir, (*Voice rising.*) it's so
stupid, and then she was (*Indicates where*
LOUISE *was sitting.*) talking about it just
now, I mean I've *had* to think about it so
much (*Fast, he looks at* KRAMER.) How
did you guess sir?

KRAMER: It happens all the time Stephen
– I've known it happen so often. (*Without
a break into the radio:*) Have you found
him yet? You've got just two minutes to
find him. (*Straight back to* STEPHEN.)
Go on.

STEPHEN: It's very difficult not to think of
them, all the time ... in a hot bundle, and
she making all that noise for him.

KRAMER (*into the radio*): No I mean that,
it's very important. (*Immediately:*) You
can go on if you want Stephen – if you
want to tell me.

STEPHEN (*fast, pouring out*): And you
know when you're on a job at night – the
lads chatting away, larking around in the
front seat, you know, really noisily and
dirty laughter and you see the girls
looking up from outside the discos like
they *know* all about it. You almost want
to kill them. It's difficult sir, you can
hardly think, and you get back, four, five,
in the morning, and she doesn't even
wake up when you get in beside her, her
skin feels different, I don't know how to
describe it, but warm in a different way,
and she sleeps like she's been walking in
the desert or somewhere for a year.

KRAMER: She's only a kid – she can be
taught.

Spattered barracking in the distance.

STEPHEN: I nearly went to our Welfare

Officer.

KRAMER (*into the walkie-talkie*): No I
don't! (*Turns.*) He's a complete idiot, a
waste of money, all police Welfare
Officers are jokes, all the ones I've ever
met – they're totally out of touch, useless.
No you did right to tell me Stephen. You
must always tell me things. I am the
person to come to, anytime you want,
because I am the one who can do
something.

STEPHEN: I know sir – thank you. It's
good to know that, I could only come to
you. (*Excited very fast:*) I know a lot of
the lads feel the same, I mean they do
very, (*Embarrassed.*) you know, look up
to you sir. I mean you go into a station
after you've been on a visit sir and they're
all talking about you, and trying to copy
you sir. I hope things don't go wrong for
you tonight.

KRAMER (*sharp*): No. (*Glances at*
STEPHEN.) You really shouldn't worry
about it; sex couldn't be less important in
the end, it just does not matter.
Concentrate on your career, I may help
you from time to time. (*Into the radio:*)
Yes that's the one. Well get him out of
there! I don't care, I need him, get him
out!

STEPHEN (*who is trying to pull the cork out
again, strong pull*): Christ this one doesn't
want to come either. (*Pulls.*) Fuck it, I
don't know what's the matter with them.

KRAMER (*slight grin*): The *bottles* won't
even open for us.

STEPHEN (*his voice changes, pulling at the
bottle really hard so that his knuckles
shine*): But it's just you see sir – I do
rather like her still, it's stupid really, but I
do want her to stay, *I want her to stay with
me*, because I do so like her . . .

*He suddenly bursts into tears on this last
line, choking them back almost
immediately as he realises* CAROLINE *is
there and watching.*

KRAMER: No let it come out. Go on. Let
it all come out.

STEPHEN *cries.*

It doesn't matter about her, she will have
seen people cry before. (*His voice is quiet,
matter of fact.*) I don't mind people letting
it come out in private, letting their

feelings go, it's in public I won't have my
men misbehaving. I've seen fifty year old
men breakdown, hold onto one's arm, go
down on their knees in front of me.

KRAMER *glances at* STEPHEN, *a very
slight distant touch on his shoulder. The
bleep of his radio goes.*

KRAMER (*into the radio*): That's right.
(*To* STEPHEN:) OK I think that's
enough. (*Smiles.*) One can have too much
of a good thing!

STEPHEN *grins at this through a tear
spattered face.*

STEPHEN: Yes I know. (*He smiles.*)
Thank you very much sir.

KRAMER: Here. (*He hands him a clean
white handkerchief, smiles.*) I'm giving
them away tonight.

*The handclap in the distance is growing
much louder.*

STEPHEN (*takes the handkerchief, but is
already trying the bottle*): I'm going to do
it this time.

He pulls the cork. He laughs.

It's coming – I'VE DONE IT.

*The cork comes out, white foam pouring
out of the champagne bottle. He giggles
nervously again at the foam.*

Oh Christ! Look at it – sorry sir, that's
very vulgar, I mustn't start again . . .

KRAMER: No you mustn't.

STEPHEN (*pouring a drink for
KRAMER*): I can't remember seeing you
drink sir – the other times I've driven you.

KRAMER (*looks down at the glass*): Yes
I'd forgotten what it looked like too.

Barracking applause now very sharp.

I don't know if I like the sound of that!

STEPHEN (*staring out across the barbed
wire*): The whole place is not going to go
up – is it sir?

KRAMER (*very slight pause*): Of course
not – not a chance.

(*Walkie-talkie noise.*) Good! Not before
time! (*To* STEPHEN *indicating*
CAROLINE:) Look after our friend,
give her a glass. (*Back into the walkie-
talkie, he paces backwards and forwards,*

adrenalin really churning:) OK! Are you the compère? Good. My name is Kramer, I'm the Chief Constable . . . I want you to announce *Mister David* yes, the small horror with white hair, is going up there to perform in precisely ten minutes, that's right. I said ANNOUNCE IT . . . I don't care if you don't know where he is, I'm going to have to find him . . . yes . . . if I have to tear the grass off the field to do it . . . he's the only thing we've got . . . *listen* – I'm telling you, announce it (*Slight smile.*) that's an order.

He clicks off the radio, wipes his hair back, moves restlessly – the barracking is sharp and loud.

IF he doesn't do it now, I'll go up there; myself and shout it out. (*He stares at* CAROLINE.) You've put on weight since we started.

CAROLINE: Since I've hardly eaten anything all day – that would have been clever.

KRAMER (*slight smile*): You minded being told that . . . (*He swings round.*) Stephen! – check back to HQ, see if they've got anybody sitting on their arses, who they can send over, I might just need them. And be quick. (*Flicks round to* CAROLINE.) Are you cold?

CAROLINE (*surprised*): A little.

KRAMER: And bring the lady one of my sleeveless sweaters (*He looks at her.*) I use the car as a second home . . . You should have stayed in Peterborough shouldn't you – you would have been better off having a Saturday night skating wouldn't you? (*He looks straight at her.*) Don't you think?

CAROLINE: No I don't. (*Smiles, glancing towards barracking applause in distance.*) Perhaps *you* should have stayed at home.

KRAMER (*as if he hadn't heard*): What was that mumble? You'd never be any good in a witness box would you . . . ? (*Glances restlessly over his shoulder.*) I was terrified out of my wits my first time – I spoke with more of an accent in those days, I was a shy kid, the Judge kept on saying speak up Constable nobody can hear you . . . Come on!

Immediately the noise of the tannoy is heard in the distance, but quite loud.

SIMON'S VOICE (*through the tannoy*): Good news friends, all being well in ten minutes or so Mister David will perform, and our interrupted evening – or night as it is now – will be resumed in really fine style, with one of the most exciting sights around at the moment.

Cat calls, and cheers in the distance then the noise lessens greatly.

KRAMER (*turns*): Did I tell him to say *about* ten minutes? Did you hear me say that? (*Into the walkie-talkie, very sharp:*) OK, right! Now tell him if he goes anywhere near a microphone again tonight, he'll be eating it for his cooked breakfast tomorrow . . .

He clicks off the radio.

CAROLINE (*watching him*): That's a risk isn't it – you don't even know where Mister David is.

KRAMER (*standing still*): He'll come up here – to me. He won't be able to resist coming, after hearing that.

CAROLINE: But he won't do anything for you, will he?

KRAMER: I only take risks I win. I was famous for being a very bad loser at school – smarted about it for months.

CAROLINE: And if he doesn't come?

KRAMER (*very quiet*): Then I've got trouble. (*Pause. Sharp:*) Do you believe in him – this kid – does he do it for real?

CAROLINE: Yes, I think so.

STEPHEN *emerges from the car where he's been radioing.*

KRAMER (*loud*): Well?

STEPHEN (*moving up from the car*): They say they haven't got a single person that can come.

KRAMER (*hardly showing his disappointment*): I didn't think they would. It was a long shot. Give her that. (*Indicates the sweater.*) Then give me *another* drink.

STEPHEN *very surprised, takes his glass to refill.*

STEPHEN: But the chopper's coming now sir.

Noise in the distance of a helicopter which

grows louder quickly and passes by, though not directly overhead.

KRAMER (*turning towards the black cyclorama, and looking up*): Yes there she is . . . somewhere . . . not low enough though – I wanted her lower.

STEPHEN *hands him his drink.*

Pour yourself one.

STEPHEN *moves to the table and gingerly helps himself.*

CAROLINE (*she has put on his sweater*): It must be strange being able to produce helicopters out of the sky like that, when you want.

KRAMER (*matter of fact*): It has its uses.

Noise of the chopper dying away.

I like them.

CAROLINE: It won't be able to see very much though . . .

KRAMER: But it'll take their minds off things – for a few useful moments.

CAROLINE: You think that will stop people going berserk. (*Up by the barbed wire fence, her hand moving restlessly.*)

KRAMER: People have only come to this glittering occasion to prove to themselves they're still alive.

He looks at CAROLINE.

Haven't they?

CAROLINE: I don't think I need any proof. (*Insolent smile.*) But maybe you do?

KRAMER: Don't become rude young lady, that would be stupid. And I don't think you are stupid – one of the brighter youngsters I've met, in some ways.

CAROLINE: So I've earned a compliment now. Perhaps I'll get offered a lift soon. You're really quite worried aren't you? (KRAMER *turns surprised.*) You're going to have a riot on your hands aren't you? And It's going to be an ugly one.

Applause and noise in the distance.

KRAMER (*slight smile*): I don't think so. If no mistakes are made nothing ever goes wrong.

CAROLINE: But you've already made one.

KRAMER: Now I've told you don't go too far, or I'll have you moved. (*He watches her.*) It's unusual meeting an aggressive typist.

CAROLINE (*smiles*): Is it? You'll be wanting me to take dictation next . . .

Slight pause – applause continuing.

KRAMER: What was the mistake?

CAROLINE: You went up on stage, uninvited, and made a personal appearance – and that provoked trouble, not stopped it.

Tense pause.

KRAMER: I don't think you'll find that so.

He moves hand, beating his side with real impatience.

CAROLINE: One person's been stabbed already.

KRAMER (*staring at her wearing his sweater*): Does that fit you?

CAROLINE: Not quite, no.

KRAMER: But it rather suits you. (*Then a sharp order to* STEPHEN:) Find out if there's any sign of him yet.

STEPHEN *picks up the walkie-talkie.*

CAROLINE (*direct at him*): You're going to keep me here for as long as you can – aren't you?

KRAMER: Am I?

CAROLINE: Yes – and I don't know why. It can't be for my company . . .

KRAMER: You don't have to worry.

CAROLINE (*louder*): Why are you? (*He remains impassive.*) You believe me presumably – you must have realised I had nothing to do with those drugs.

KRAMER: I'll be seeing to you shortly . . . (*Slight smile.*) You have a ringside seat, haven't you, something to tell your friends about – in coffee breaks.

CAROLINE: As long as I can walk away at the end without alarms going off and berserk policemen chasing me. (*Loud.*) You shouldn't look away when people are talking to you.

KRAMER *has moved, he turns and stares straight at her.*

KRAMER: Did I tell you I had a daughter?

CAROLINE: You know you did.

KRAMER (*staring at her*): Yes – she's got fair hair, large round face, very pale blue eyes, large bust. A quiet girl, she's very docile. I know everything about her, every inch. Sometimes I look up and stare at her across the breakfast table and wonder what's going on in her head. I watch – and then I tell her what she's thinking. I'm usually right . . .

CAROLINE: And how do you know you are?

KRAMER: Because she tells me. (*He looks at her.*) It's very easy to know what kids are thinking and wanting now.

CAROLINE: Can you tell me what *I'm* thinking now?

Very slight pause.

KRAMER: Yes of course.

He stares at her, she's disconcerted under his gaze, looks away for a second, and then at him.

(*His tone changes:*) And it's not very printable is it . . .

KEN *has entered with* DAVID – *holding* DAVID *by the sleeve – who stands quite still by his side.* KRAMER *turns to him.*

You found him!

KEN: Yes – he was making his way up here by himself.

KRAMER (*looking at* DAVID): Yes I know he was.

KEN (*surprised*): Really? – And he says he's not going on – to perform under any circumstances.

KRAMER: I see.

He looks straight at DAVID.

Can't he speak for himself? – You're not his ventriloquist's dummy.

DAVID *does not reply.*

(*Sharp:*) Stephen – give Mister David a glass of wine.

DAVID *stands completely still.*

I'm sure he drinks wine. (*To* DAVID:) Don't you? Do you want a drink, a glass of Mr Richard's champagne?

DAVID *doesn't move.*

Go on pour him one.

Glances at CAROLINE.

And you can fill hers up too.

CAROLINE (*sharp*): She's had enough thank you . . .

KEN (*moving up to* KRAMER *confidentially, urgently*): They've got the stabbed kid off now – he'll need to be sewn up . . . the lights on the north perimeter have blown or been vandalised, if you want my advice . . .

KRAMER (*quiet*): It's possible I don't Ken.

KEN: You'll send everyone home –

KRAMER *doesn't react.*

George!

KRAMER (*slight smile*): I heard you.

STEPHEN *is holding a glass of champagne.*

Go on give it to him, he'll drink it up.

DAVID *takes the glass, and holds it, standing completely still.*

(*To* DAVID:) There you are.

KEN (*louder, sharper*): There's already been trouble – we won't be able to hold them if there's any large scale violence, we'd be severely hampered by the crowd density, which is far too heavy, a lot of people could get injured . . .

KRAMER: Thank you Ken – for that. You know you don't have to use jargon to impress me, it doesn't come naturally to you. (*Looking straight at him.*) I know you know your job.

(*To* DAVID *who hasn't touched his glass:*)

Go on drink it.

KEN: As the officer who drew up the arrangements for crowd control at this festival – I feel it's my duty . . .

KRAMER (*gently*): But I'm in charge now, aren't I?

KEN (*loud*): With all due respect there have been a lot of irregularities since you arrived, like that girl being kept up here the whole time.

KRAMER (*calmly*): I don't often believe in regularities they tend to be unsuccessful.

KEN: IF we told them to pack up now, we could have a controlled walk to the station – it's only a mile, (*Loud:*) don't you realise there's a lot of black kids out there now who are very restless, its *obvious* what we've got to do before it's too late . . .

KRAMER: I don't think that's a very advisable tone to take . . .

KEN: I know you're not in the habit of listening George to anything . . .

KRAMER: I think I've always been a particularly good listener. (*Steely.*) I've heard what you've got to say Ken and that's enough, I will not tolerate public quarrels –

KEN: There are normal procedures on those occasions – and I think I can say I've had rather more experience . . .

KRAMER: I don't like the word procedure very much either . . .

KEN: Don't you (*Losing his temper, voice beginning to explode:*) With all due respect George, you're a fucking *idiot.* It's my lads down there and if my men . . . I'm telling you this

KRAMER *looks away.*

Listen will you! IF my men get hurt because of you wanting to prove something, your private schemes or whatever your're trying to do I warn you . . .

KRAMER: Ken . . .

KEN (*really shouts*): WILL YOU LISTEN. You can't always do everything on your own for Chrissake, without any consultation, disregarding everybody as if they didn't exist – can't you ever realise this is not a one man band you get worse and worse every week now, I've watched you. (*Suddenly.*) Going up on stage like that just now – totally unasked – and making absurd personal appearances! I hate your methods – the embarrassing incompetent exhibitionism of it all. You're not even meant to be here tonight are you? (*Urgent:*) I mean you realise you could have a hundred men in casualty by the end of tonight, you have no right to risk that – when it's completely, absolutely unnecessary, and I'm telling you . . . (*Shouts:*) WILL YOU LOOK AT ME, if my men get hurt, if *any* of them get hurt tonight, I will personally see a full report goes in to the chief H.M.I. with the facts,

with all THE FACTS, and I doubt if you will be Chief Constable much longer – (*Straight at him:*) for Chrissake you just cannot go on running things like you are.

Silence.

KRAMER (*into the radio*): A car for Superintendent Daniels. Yes. He'll meet it at the bottom of the hill.

He looks at KEN.

Go home to bed Ken, you're relieved of your duties for the night . . .

KEN (*looking straight back at him*): I knew that's what you would do – you had to . . .

KRAMER: Go on, home to bed, that's an order.

KEN: The Kramer Way . . . (*He moves.*) I'll take my own car thank you.

He goes.

KRAMER (*watching after him for a split second*): He's forgotten his sleeping pod.

STEPHEN *stands by* DAVID – CAROLINE *watching him.*

I've seen that man walking in the park with a girl of seventeen picked up from the canteen at Bridge Street. Her hair in a ponytail and he running after her through the playground. It's sad when grown men make fools of themselves like that. He's not a bad policeman.

DAVID *carefully turns his glass upside down and pours champagne onto the ground.*

Fine! I'll pour him another. Put our friend in the car Stephen.

He looks at CAROLINE.

You don't mind sitting there for a few minutes.

CAROLINE: But I thought I was having a ringside seat?

STEPHEN *leads* CAROLINE *to the car.*

KRAMER: And wind up the windows. (*After* CAROLINE:) You're to behave yourself inside it.

CAROLINE *sits in the car,* STEPHEN *winds up the window.*

Find Mr Richards and tell him I'll be down there in five minutes *with* Mister David.

STEPHEN: Right sir!

STEPHEN *goes.*
KRAMER *turns alone with DAVID on stage who stands absolutely still, occasionally blinking.*

You've been a little hard to find you know . . .

DAVID (*glances behind him – then looks back*): Are you talking to me?

KRAMER (*filling his champagne glass*): There's nobody else here is there.

DAVID (*staring back, big innocent eyes*): There's you . . .

KRAMER (*staring at him across the width of the stage*): We're not going to play games I'm afraid. Did you hear the announcement that went out over the Public Address just now?

DAVID: No – I didn't hear anything.

KRAMER: You're going up on stage to perform in four and a half minutes . . .

DAVID (*totally blank*): Who you talking to?

KRAMER (*holding his champagne glass*): So I think you better get ready.

DAVID: HE won't be talked to like that.

KRAMER (*puzzled for a second*): Who?

DAVID *blinks.*

Because you see you've been officially announced.

DAVID (*very sharp*): Did you hear what I just said – he *won't* be talked to like that.

KRAMER (*totally calm*): And very soon you'll only have four minutes.

DAVID (*very sharp his small figure standing there*): I'll give you one last chance – did you or did you not hear what I said?

KRAMER: I did.

DAVID: Good – then don't do it again!

KRAMER (*right up to him, presses the full glass of champagne into DAVID's hand*): You can't out-stare me, I'm afraid.

DAVID: We'll see.

KRAMER: People, believe it or not, have paid to see you.

DAVID: You're not going to go on about the breaking of contracts now are you? Surely you can do better than that.

KRAMER (*sharp*): Yes but you have signed a binding agreement . . .

DAVID (*dangerous smile, cutting him off*): I'm only a kid – how am I meant to understand those things. (*Tone changes.*) This is becoming a security matter, is it?

KRAMER (*sharp back at him*): Yes, this is not part of my normal day, but I am . . .

DAVID (*cutting him off*): You need me to go on don't you – or you'll be in real trouble (*He blinks.*) desperate trouble.

KRAMER (*keeping his cool, but sharp*): Nothing compared to what you'll be in . . .

DAVID (*cutting him off*): You're depending on me – but I won't do it. And absolutely nothing you can do will make me.

KRAMER: And what about all those people who have come . . .

DAVID (*cutting him off*): HE CAN'T HEAR YOU. (*He throws the glass across the stage and shouts:*) Can't you get that into your skull.

Pause.

You look worried. You're not doing very well, Mr Kramer. (*Dangerous smile.*) You going to try again? (*Slight pause.*)

KRAMER: You've got less than 4 minutes now and you don't want to go on unprepared presumably.

DAVID *moves off towards the exit.*

KRAMER (*quick, sudden change of tone*): Is your name really David, David?

DAVID *stops, slight grin.*

DAVID: That's a really desperate try (*Slight pause.*) Course it isn't – why should it be. It was Ian before David.

KRAMER: Yeah.

DAVID: And before that it was Jason, before that it was Harvey, before that it was Rod, you have to go back nine names to get to my real name – and you won't ever know that.

KRAMER: I thought you must have other names – (*Slight smile.*) I used to call myself Victor instead of George in private, to myself.

DAVID (*sharp*): Did you? It doesn't suit you.

KRAMER: When I was small I read the comic strips – I used to fantasise about doing peculiar striking things too, like you, and becoming famous.

Pause.

You're a fake, aren't you?

Silence. DAVID turns to the other side of the stage.

DAVID: Do you want to repeat that?

KRAMER: You fake all this breaking and lifting and moving – there's no real magic, or mystery at all, is there – you're a simple, total fake.

Slight pause.

DAVID: Have you been drinking?

KRAMER (*staring*): Aren't you?

Silence, KRAMER watches him.

DAVID (*suddenly*): Of course I fake it – how else could I possibly do it. (*Savage:*) You'd believe anything!

KRAMER: No, I never did.

DAVID (*sharp*): I did break something once of course, just by staring at it. Maybe. A huge window of a fridge shop.

DAVID looks straight at KRAMER. Pause. He folds his arms.

I don't see why you think this will help you – it's having the opposite effect.

KRAMER: And who put you up to this, David?

DAVID: Just the sort of question you would ask, isn't it! It was all me – *I decided to do it.*

KRAMER: Yes – I thought so.

DAVID: At school, in Watford! (*With disgust:*) EVER BEEN THERE? It was in the maths lesson, because it was even worse than the others. Our class room was by a motorway, so you thought a lot. (*Abstracted:*) I wanted to get out of there so much, of course.

KRAMER (*watching him carefully*): And this was the easiest way you could find.

DAVID: No – the quickest. Get right out. I wrote it down first in composition, they still called it that at our school. 'What you wanna do when you grow up, in not more than three pages.' Mine was nine pages so they didn't read half of it of course. They never found out the end. So I decided to do it properly. Break ugly things on stage just by looking at them and put in a few songs to make it new, and maybe a little violence, and a few mild shocks, and use my age to advantage. My mate helped me, we were in a band together first, he's much older than me of course, about sixteen. He's out there now, mingling with the audience.

KRAMER: He helps you fake it?

DAVID (*loud*): That word *is not permitted.* Every time you open your mouth, you make it worse for yourself. (*Loud:*) Do you realise that? (*Slight pause. Mocking:*) Your mind's racing isn't it, I can hear it clearly – What to do next!

KRAMER watching him.

KRAMER (*deciding to continue*): And why hasn't anybody found you out, David?

DAVID (*dangerous smile*): Because we're so good at it. (*Looking at him.*) The record company doesn't let anybody hostile too close. But people like the idea, anyway, the whole package, me doing it, because I'm so young, and a bit small, there's already a kid imitating me in America, (*Professional.*) I hit a sort of a nerve didn't I . . . They like a bit of escape. (*Suddenly:*) You should see the bloody letters I get, these crazy letters people send me . . .

KRAMER (*encouraging him*): Asking you to break all sorts of things.

DAVID (*suspiciously*): Yeah . . . maybe.

KRAMER: Shatter their old T.V. sets so they can be replaced, make the block of flats they're in crash down.

DAVID (*really suspicious*): Yes. As it happens.

KRAMER (*flip*): I get some letters, too.

DAVID (*suddenly loud*): One of them wrote to ask me to make the whole of the new centre of Newcastle crumble down, just by staring at it! . . . even coming here some really small kids stopped my car and wanted me to bust up their bloody awful playground – So they could have a new one. One of the girls asked me to make one of her tits bigger. All of them wanting me to do some sort of bloody stupid magic . . .

KRAMER is by DAVID's silk bag, he

moves to handle it.

DAVID (*loud*): Don't touch that! It's unlucky, don't you ever listen to anything you're told.

KRAMER (*quiet*): Not often.

DAVID *turns upstage. Barracking.*

DAVID: There'll be an inquiry if people get killed tonight won't there. Will you get the sack! Won't look good, will it – being beaten by a kid that's not yet thirteen. (*More barracking. Pause. Steely, straight at him:*) The reason you can't win is, Mr Kramer because they'll be able to tell it's not real out there.

KRAMER: No, they won't.
Just stare them straight in the face, pick a single one out and never let it go.

DAVID (*sharp*): I don't work like that.

DAVID *moves.*

KRAMER (*sharply urgent*): Listen to me. They want to believe in you – all of them out there. People aren't really very complicated, you know, even less so than when I was your age. They'll see what they want to see, and if they want a bit of magic, a bit of science fiction – then that's exactly what they'll see. It doesn't have to be real. They'll clutch on to anything. (*He smiles.*) That's why you've become a star, David. (*Slight pause.*) And we both happen to know what they want, don't we. And it's up to us now to give it to them. You've got two minutes left, plenty of time.
DAVID *has half turned to the other side of the stage.*

DAVID (*steely*): Not a bad try – the trouble is – you're too late. I'm not doing it anymore, I've given it up.

KRAMER (*chancing everything*): I think you're afraid.

DAVID: You really think insulting me is going to make a difference. (*Screams:*) Can't you *understand.* I don't like *doing it anymore. I hate it.* I don't want to go out there! I don't like live people watching.

KRAMER: So? I had to do things when I was first a policeman which I did not like, crashes, people bleeding inside cars, I really quite minded that, more than most.

Pause.

DAVID (*loud*): What's that got to do with me – that's totally different.

KRAMER: No, *it's not.* (*Sharp:*) My first violent crime, a nasty thing, a body on a railway line, in the very early morning. An old man, the arm was cut off. It was missing.

DAVID (*angry*): Why are you telling me this?

KRAMER: And because I was the youngest one there I was sent to look for it. It was lying in a loganberry bush, berries all over it, and the hand was still wearing a blue mitten. I fainted twice before I got it back to the others. I was covered head to foot in mud. I looked like a black and white minstrel. A kid of eighteen – I didn't start as young as you – holding a severed arm and trying to smile with the others.

DAVID (*no sign of emotion*): So, you were scared, were you?

KRAMER (*cooly*): But it's rather a magnificent feeling when you master it, triumph through it, (*Lightly:*) it makes you feel you can achieve almost anything. Now you can show me the very worst things, and it has no effect on me at all. Do you see?

Silence.

DAVID (*quiet*): You don't have to talk down to me, like I'm a child.

KRAMER: Yes (*Slight smile.*) I'd noticed you're not. What are you doing?

DAVID (*takes out a walkie-talkie and begins strapping it round himself*): Packing up.

KRAMER (*surprised*): You've got one of those!

DAVID (*strapping it round his pale bare chest*): Yes. Why not? When I'm doing it, it goes round like this, and I link up with my contact on the ground, my mate. It's called wiring up.

He pulls the aeriel up: it snaps off in his hand.

DAVID (*angry*): Oh Christ! It's broken. Like a matchstick – just snapped off.

KRAMER: See, you can really break things after all.

DAVID (*sharp*): That's right.

KRAMER: It'll still work – you needn't worry.

DAVID: Will it?

KRAMER, *uncertain whether* DAVID's *decided to go on.*

KRAMER: You *can* do it (*Lightly.*) I'm counting on you, David.

DAVID (*stares at him*): I know. (*Suddenly really loud.*) I wanna sit in the car – I wanna drive it.

KRAMER: Afterwards – after you've performed, you can sit in front.

DAVID: *No, I've got to now.*

KRAMER (*very loud*): NO. (DAVID *turns.*) YOU WILL DO AS YOU'RE TOLD.

Tense moment. DAVID *turns to face him.*

DAVID (*suddenly, direct and vulnerable*): And what if it goes wrong? It'll be really terrifying tonight.

KRAMER: It won't. (*Soothingly:*) It's one of the best feelings in the world facing a crowd, I've faced big violent demonstrations and the moment when they go strangely quiet, a mass of blurred hostile faces, all staring straight at you, and wanting something sharp and simple from you, that is the most exciting silence there is.

DAVID (*looking straight at him, his manner sharp again*): If it goes wrong you're going to come falling down with me. (*Steely:*) Do you understand.

STEPHEN *enters with a kid of about seventeen,* STEPHEN *holding on to him.*

KRAMER (*swings round*): Mister David is going to perform!

STEPHEN: Good sir.

KRAMER (*glancing at the kid*): Who's he?

STEPHEN: He was found with a knife on him sir. They think he might have done that other kid, he's not saying anything.

KRAMER: Take him straight down.

STEPHEN: Yes sir – there's a car waiting. But I thought you'd want to see him.

KRAMER: Quite right – yes.

STEPHEN: And he wanted to speak to you . . .

KRAMER (*looks round – straight at the boy, slight pause*): OK – let him stay and watch the show. (*To the* KID:) Do you want to watch it.

KID: Yeah . . . ok.

KRAMER (*sharp*): Sir . . .

KID: Sir.

KRAMER (*leading* DAVID *to the exit*): The Boy's going on.

He flicks his hands towards the car.

Let her out of the car now.

STEPHEN (*to* DAVID): Good luck.

KRAMER *is going out and* STEPHEN *is leading the kid towards the police car. He lets* CAROLINE *out.* NIGEL *and* LOUISE *run on.*

NIGEL (*calls out*): Hey . . . wait.

STEPHEN: The boy's going on – he's getting ready sir.

NIGEL: Is he! Thank god.

Both NIGEL *and* LOUISE *are far too preoccupied to take in the kid.* STEPHEN *goes off with* CAROLINE *and the* KID.

NIGEL: So now we just have to hold our breath.

LOUISE: And hope it works. A lot's resting on that child.

NIGEL (*sharp*): That's an understatement. (*He moves.*) Maybe I could have organised things better . . . No I don't think so. I can't really see how. (*Pause.*) You can't *trust* anyone.

LOUISE (*looking at him*): You've just been a little amateurish really haven't you.

NIGEL: Amateurish!

LOUISE: Yes.

NIGEL: Nothing could be further from the truth. For somebody who's so bright you do say some amazingly stupid things. (*Slight pause, his tone genuine:*) You know how hard I worked on this (*He looks at her, genuine.*) Didn't I?

LOUISE: Yes. (*Gently but firmly:*) I just don't want you to be hurt by tonight – held responsible if . . .

NIGEL: I won't be.

LOUISE (*gently*): You will be.

NIGEL *looking at her, taken aback by her strength.*

NIGEL: Why on earth did you come out with all that stuff while we were drinking.

LOUISE: I don't know.

NIGEL (*sharp*): It was an extraordinary thing to do.

LOUISE (*moving*): It doesn't really matter very much right at this moment, does it?

She is under the tree, NIGEL watching her.

NIGEL (*quieter*): We met under a tree.

LOUISE: You think I've forgotten that. (*She glances at him.*) You were sort of draped against it . . . looking rather startling . . . even slightly frightening (*Slight pause.*) until one got up close.

NIGEL: Did I?

LOUISE (*slight smile to herself*): You were very authoritative about a great many things that night, under that tree.

LOUISE *moves again, glancing towards where the noise comes from.*

Christ – I hope people don't get violent. That would be so terrible. People have been killed on occasions like this, haven't they . . . trampled and things . . . (*Slight pause.*) Think what that would mean if people were killed . . .

NIGEL: It won't happen tonight – I think. (*Gentler.*) Do you want me to take you home, love?

LOUISE (*looking straight back at him*): I think you really ought to stay, don't you? You wouldn't leave your own party, would you, Nigel?

NIGEL: No, of course not. (*Suddenly, fondly.*) I'm glad you're here.

LOUISE: I know you are.

They look at each other for a second.

NIGEL: I don't trust that boy if he really is a boy – which I'm beginning to have severe doubts about. If only he'll just . . . (*He stops.*) I hope he . . .

LOUISE (*suddenly*): We've got to go and watch – make him. We can't just dangle

around up here while he's on, come on, now – (*Sharper:*) Come on, Nigel.

They go.

The music is loud – the stage rumbles on – as it moves into place we hear loud through tannoy the voice of an electrician, very flat: 'Testing, testing, one two three, half a pound of twopenny rice, half a pound of treacle'. Suddenly there is a loud drum roll and then we hear NIGEL's voice.

NIGEL'S VOICE (*through tannoy*): Ladies and Gentlemen. Friends welcome . . . MISTER DAVID.

Off-stage applause. Bright light bursts onto the platform stage. DAVID walks into spot as a loud piercing fanfare sounds, followed by a moment of total silence.

DAVID is wearing a cloak, black with scarlet lining, and shining spangled boots, no cap on his white hair. He holds his red silk bag. The platform stage has been set with household goods, large hideous vases and coloured glass bowls on a table, an electric cooker, a toaster, several television sets, two pieces of concrete. Music starts, he mimes to the sound of a heavy rock backing track over which comes the sound of a boy soprano singing 'Oh For the Wings of a Dove'. The rock music eventually drowns it out.

DAVID: You thought I was singing, didn't you?

DAVID stands very still as the music swells up, staring into the audience. Suddenly he takes out of the red silk bag three heavy metal bars, places them quickly on the floor. He picks one up then throws it down with a terrific clang, picks another one up, turns round very quickly, his small face up to the microphone.

DAVID: Watch! I said watch!

He lifts a 'metal' bar up in front of him as the music rises, touches it, it snaps in two. He holds the pieces up, loud applause. He turns and weaves round the stage fast, picks up the concrete bar and places it on the table, but then suddenly he crosses back to the microphone, his movements very professional and seemingly very confident, and sings the verse of a song in a sharp clear little voice to a tape accompaniment, he sings just one verse, and then as the music continues to play, he turns from the microphone and falls flat on his face. He lies there for a split second as the music fades out, then jumps up confidently, grinning, we realise it was an act.

DAVID (*loud*): You thought that was an accident! You did – I saw you. Yes I saw *you.* But it was to prove to you I'm not carrying any electrical aids.

He smiles a forced smile.

Silence now, absolute silence.

He turns, then back into the mike.

I SAID SILENCE.

He glances towards the table.

I'm going to break these vases now.

He points to the biggest of the vases.

Because I don't like them at all – they don't deserve to be here!

The music changes – he stares at the vase.

Break!

The vase doesn't break. He faces the wall of consumer objects on stage.

(*An automatic professional smile.*) I have to hate it you see. Break!

(*The vase doesn't break – he raises his voice:*) It will – now!

The vase shatters – DAVID smiles with relief. Two more vases shatter immediately afterwards.

DAVID (*stands centre stage and shouts into the microphone*): You see I can do it!

He takes out a strange pair of spectacles and puts them on, green and black lenses and hideously shaped rims. He holds out his hands in front of him, blind fashion.

DAVID: You see! I can't see anything.

DAVID *faces out as the music plays quietly under him.*

There is a man, with fair hair, right back, under the willow tree and . . . and

His manner falters slightly.

and he's called Keith, that's his name, and he's just been talking about his mother and her boyfriend who's got a lisp, and there's a stone in his . . . in his left plimsoll which is hurting him and he's taking it

out. (*Loud:*) Right?

The music cuts out for a second waiting for the reply and we hear a distant shouted 'right' – immediately the music starts again as applause comes up – DAVID moves as if rushing to get it over.

Watch now. Quiet – I want quiet. I can move this cooker now.

He stares at the shiny electric cooker – his voice brisk, rushing through the act.

I can move it – because I hate it. Go on.

The cooker refuses to move.

Go on, move. It will move for me, right round the stage – (*To the cooker:*) You're going to – go on. You're going to move. I can make it dance if I want.

The cooker doesn't move, he crosses over and puts an electric toaster on top of the cooker.

It'll do it now – watch. (*He shouts at it:*) Move. (*It doesn't move.*) You think this isn't meant to happen don't you. (*Voice rising:*) But it's going to move! Now!

Music rising to crescendo – he suddenly moves up to it.

Go on you bloody thing.

He gives it a violent kick, and then turns, forced confident smile as catcalls come up. He immediately begins rolling out some large metal balls from behind the table.

I can split these open, watch I can.

He stares down at the steel balls.

Go on!

Nothing happens – the music is loud. He glances desperately into wings.

I can break the television, watch – it broke easily before!

The T.V. doesn't break. He stares desperately at the wall of television sets.

(*He screams:*) I can break anything!

He stares at the other vases on the tables, catcalls loud. He picks up a plate and smashes it by hand on the side of table.

Shit! (*Furious it's going wrong. Loud catcalls, he tries to smile:*) Watch (*Louder:*) Watch me.

He lifts the microphone stand high above

his head, he is beginning to shake with tears and real nerves.

See I – I can make this knife melt. I can! – or break – or . . . I CAN.

He drops it onto the floor, catcalls or slow handclap very loud. DAVID *sits down in the middle of the stage, glances into the wings.*

Can I have a towel please?

He glances round, clenched.

DAVID: This isn't on purpose.

He looks round – the music stops.

Can somebody give me a towel please?

DAVID *looks over his shoulder.* KRAMER *walks onto the stage.*

KRAMER: OK – the kid's a bit tired, he did well didn't he. He's been waiting in the wings quite a while.

DAVID *is sitting at his feet.*

He didn't finish, but he's given his best. (*Louder:*) Given all he could.

He picks up a piece of snapped 'metal' off the stage.

This is really broken.

He puts it in his pocket. He lifts DAVID *up by the arm – the crowd is already falling quiet, chastened by the sight of the defeated child. In the following speech* KRAMER *rides on the back of that reaction.*

And let's see a smile from him – that's right.

A tiny, very nervous smile from DAVID.

A bit more – good. Go and get yourself a wash now and a cup of strong tea – you deserve it.

DAVID *glances at* KRAMER *and goes.*

KRAMER *is alone on the stage by the microphone.*

They asked me to put make-up on – but you've got the real unadorned thing. Pale it maybe but it's real.

He puts the sword down – sharp, we feel the adrenalin, he's thinking quickly.

KRAMER: Now you all haven't done too badly so far – against expectations. (*Loud:*) And it's going to be kept that

way. You may not like me very much – and I may not, very probably don't, like you. But I'm here, now, and I'm not going to be easily moved. (*Loud:*) We're going to have absolutely no more bother. I don't like violence and nor do you in your brighter moments – so there's going to be no arsing around out there. NONE. I know all about it – I've had my 'fun' too in the past, I was brought up on the streets, I know it all. I can remember running on the pavements kicking people from behind, tripping up fat women as they were shopping, head over heels into the litter bins, but believe me this is rather better – rather more satisfying (*Shouts:*) I will not have any more trouble tonight. Policemen also bleed you know as the song says and much more easily than people suppose. I know what a lot of you are thinking. I can see it very easily from here. Don't. (*Loud:*) Just don't. I will not let it happen tonight – and if anyone here tries to hurt anyone else, I will make certain that person will not enjoy life again for a very long time. (*Quieter:*) I just will not let you be selfish. And if you're wondering if he really means what he says, I don't advise you to put it to the test. (*He takes his jacket off.*

Suddenly fast:) Give me a P
Give me an E
Give me an A
Give me a C
Give me an E
Peace

(*Slight grin.*) Lucky I learnt to spell isn't it. That's right. And as a reward for this – you've paid your money I know, and some of you haven't got too much of it, and you've travelled from all corners of the country – as a reward you have the greatest, the most live, the most exciting event there is to offer, coming now. Something a lot of you may have never seen before in your short or not so short lives – the morning coming up. Yes, you heard me right despite the look of surprise. That's exactly what I said. Sunrise. And we're going to help it on its way with a bit of music. You've never seen it like you're going to see it now; most of you city kids, city folk, will never have seen it before at all. Some of you are thinking – I can hear it clearly – is that all he has to offer us, that's not interesting, that's not enough. People trying to feel let

down. But YOU ARE WRONG. I'm
awake and driving every dawn of the year
– I see it break every day – and I can tell
you it's the most beautiful sight in the
world. Natural and God-given. We've got
a splendid clear sky, totally empty, which
is pure luck. Everything's set for it. That's
what is coming up for you, and you will
not be disappointed. I can assure you.
And you're going to be quiet, really quiet,
because it's very possible you may not get
another chance for quite a while. I said
quiet. I know a lot of you have cramp,
sore skin, been bitten by insects, and spilt
your drinks – but now relax that tense
body, open those smoked-filled lungs,
and let all that fitlh pour out, all the
greyness and overtiredness, and breathe
this air in, let it go right the way through
you. (*Tone changes.*) When it comes it
may make you feel rather small. Give you
a chance to think about what you are
doing, where you are going, and how
much it's cost you – what will happen
when you get up from here and walk away
– a chance to look into your inside and
why not? You haven't done that for quite
some while have you really, some of you
can close your eyes right up until the
moment you feel the warmth, the light
actually touch you, your face. We're
going to see it together in one large, large
body, hardly moving, hardly speaking.
Here it comes then, very soon. God bless
you.

He walks off the stage – no catcalls.

*Music starts, loud and confident. He walks
off the platform stage, and stands stage
left, lit as he dabs his mouth with a handkerchief and glances up towards the still
black cyclorama which is revealed as the
platform stage is moved off and the music
fades into the distance. STEPHEN and the
KID, and CAROLINE are facing him,
they haven't moved.*

STEPHEN: Well done sir. That was terrific.
You really did well!

KRAMER (*sharp*): Yes it was OK – could
have been better. (*To* CAROLINE:)
Were *you* listening?

CAROLINE (*smiles*): I couldn't really
avoid it, could I? It'll get light very soon
will it?

KRAMER: Yes – I've timed it exactly.

CAROLINE (*smiles*): Of course.

KRAMER (*slight smile*): It was the only
thing I had left.

STEPHEN: The lad wants to say something
to you sir.

KRAMER: Yes. (*He focuses on the lad.*)
He's been cautioned?

STEPHEN: Of course.

KRAMER (*to the* KID): Go ahead then.

KID (*very nervous*): You know what
happened earlier, the trouble . . . I did it.
It was me. (*Loud:*) I couldn't see that's
why. He was in the way, kept on standing
up, I couldn't see anything. I asked him to
move – but he just wouldn't so I gave it to
him.

Slight pause.

KRAMER: That's what you wanted to say
to me?

KID: Yeah.

KRAMER: Sir.

KID: Sir . . . you see I walked here from
Southampton. Couldn't get a lift and the
trains cost a lot. I really wanted to be
here. I walked a long way. (*Loud:*) And
then I couldn't see any of it!

KRAMER: But you feel better for having
told me?

KID: Yeah . . . sir. I do.

KRAMER: Good.

LOUISE *enters with* NIGEL, JOHN
following slightly behind holding
DAVID's *sleeve – we hear* LOUISE's
laughter before she enters.

LOUISE (*as she enters, to the others*): Come
on! Come on! He's here. We've found
him. (*To* KRAMER *smiling:*) Hello,
we're back.

KRAMER: Just wait a moment.

LOUISE (*laughing*): Right, of course.

KRAMER: This kid is just telling us it was
he who caused the trouble earlier.

LOUISE: He's the one who did the knifing?
You've got him as well!

KRAMER (*to the* KID): Go on.

KID (*glancing at all the others staring at him
to* KRAMER): I just wanted to tell you

. . . because I saw you up there . . . (*Urgent.*) and I've been in a bit of trouble before you see – and so I wanted to tell you myself, about it.

KRAMER: You did right to tell me. You realise you hurt somebody badly and you will be punished extremely severely because you must never do it again.

LOUISE (*staring at the KID, fascinated*): He's so young isn't he.

Pause.

KRAMER (*indicating DAVID to the KID*) Do you want his autograph before you go?

KID (*surprised*): Oh yeah. OK. Thanks.

KRAMER *hands a biro and paper to LOUISE who hands it to DAVID and watches him sign.*

KID (*urgent*): I mean you will remember me, will you – sir!

KRAMER: I never forget anybody (*To STEPHEN:*) OK hand it to him.

STEPHEN *gets the paper.*

KID: Can I have yours too, sir?

KRAMER: Mine?

A very slight pause then he signs it.

All right you can go now – (*To STEPHEN:*) take him down and then return here.

As the KID passes him KRAMER gives him a detached look.

We may see what we can do for you.

STEPHEN *and the KID go.*

NIGEL (*smiles broadly*): My congratulations. You seem to have done it.

LOUISE: *Seem* to!

She laughs, moving near KRAMER.

You are – you are so clever! (*Loud:*) Isn't he.

She nearly touches him but then doesn't.

(*A huge smile.*) He's so bloody clever isn't he!

NIGEL: Yes. I didn't mean to mince words. You have been exceptionally skilful.

LOUISE (*giggles*) Skilful . . .

JOHN (*quiet with feeling*): It was fantastic – that's what you mean.

NIGEL: Yes it was rather (*He smiles.*) Bloody amazing in fact! I mean what's so terrific is the morning HAS to arrive, one thing that does, nothing can stop that.

KRAMER (*to CAROLINE*): You think I've forgotten you – but I haven't. (*He smiles.*) Far from it.

NIGEL (*by the remainder of the food, pulling off the muslin*): And one can forget about *them*. Thank God at last!

He throws a huge amount of food in the air – the table is violated..

At least I hope one can.

LOUISE (*her manner incredibly volatile*): I feel so . . . I feel so, you know almost, amazing as it may seem, happy. (*Quickly to KRAMER:*) I was so excruciatingly nervous and embarassed, I mean when David started to go wrong, I ran right into the middle of the wood, to hide I suppose. I'm covered with burrs or whatever they're called. See (*She touches burrs stuck to her dress.*) I don't think that's ever happened before. Not since I was small (*Laughs.*) I'm not sure I know how to get them out.

JOHN (*tweeking her dress*): You pull. Go on – really pull at them.

LOUISE (*looking at JOHN for a second*): I can even stand next to him (*She moves.*) – for a second.

JOHN (*nods at KRAMER, seriously*): I enjoyed that just now. It was good.

KRAMER: Thank you, thank you (*Looks at CAROLINE.*) as soon as they've gone . . .

CAROLINE (*sharp*): I look forward to it.

LOUISE (*looks at DAVID*): The poor boy's exhausted isn't he. (*She touches him.*) It must have all been really quite a huge strain on him –

KRAMER: He should have been in bed many many hours ago.

DAVID: I don't sleep much any more but I do feel just a little weird now.

LOUISE: You must do.

KRAMER (*looking straight at DAVID*): You see – not all of what he does is quite genuine.

NIGEL: Really? (*Slight smile.*) the little . . fraud . . .

LOUISE (*laughs*): I thought as much!

DAVID: You needn't worry yourselves – I'm never going to do any of that again ever probably (*He smiles straight at* KRAMER:) You can do it next time.

LOUISE: Doesn't he look so young suddenly. Rub all this off. (*She rubs at his white hair.*) Such a young face underneath.

NIGEL (*moving up to* KRAMER): You should go into politics you know. They could do with somebody like you.

KRAMER: I'm a policeman, not a politician. They trust me because of that. And they *do* trust me.

NIGEL: You should think about it. Join the Tory party. Could be Home Secretary in a few years, they haven't got anyone!

LOUISE (*up to him, nervously laughing*): You have surprised me you know. I think I may well be a little afraid of you. But it's quite a nice feeling – if you understand what I mean.

A blue flash of light flashes across the cyclorama.

(*Truly startled:*) What's that?

They look up at the cyclorama.

KRAMER: I asked them to get the lazers working.

NIGEL: God he's done everything. He must understand how they work.

LOUISE (*turns to* NIGEL): Your festival's going to be all right after all.

NIGEL (*he smiles*): So it seems. I don't really dare say anything more in case it's tempting fate.

LOUISE: Don't be silly. (*Touches him.*) You really ought to think before you speak sometimes you know Nigel.

NIGEL: Now don't start again.

LOUISE: Because you can sound just a little foolish sometimes.

NIGEL: Just . . .

LOUISE: No, it's all right, don't worry, I only half meant it. But you can sound

gigantically foolish just occasionally . . . But I can live with it, just . . .

NIGEL: Louise, *please* don't . . . (*Pulling himself free.*) I was thinking while you were up there – of a new plan. To build a sort of English Disney Land, create that, a huge fantasy palace for people to lose themselves in – escape from everything – like a movie studio full of . . .

LOUISE (*her fingers on* NIGEL*'s mouth*): Stop. Just stop. Just close it. (*She shuts his mouth.*) Tight. Then it'll be all right.

JOHN (*looks up, quiet*): You see it's just starting. You've timed it well.

The clyclorama is just beginning to get lighter, the arc lights are still blazing down.

KRAMER: (*to* CAROLINE. *Smiles*): Are you preparing yourself? Because they are going now.

He turns and faces them but LOUISE *moves over.*

LOUISE (*loud, fast*): We've got to see you again anyway. You must come to dinner. Sorry that sounds so ridiculous. Quite pathetic. I mean – I want to see you again. (*She sits on the ground.*) Oh Christ! This is really so childish, but I wish this feeling would go on. (*She bursts into tears.*)

NIGEL: Don't start crying now Louise.

LOUISE: I'm not crying. I'm not. It's just relief I expect.

NIGEL: The grass is damp now love. Please get up. You'll catch cold.

KRAMER: You're all a little overwrought. None of you have had any sleep. I think you should find a spot out there and sit with the others, and wait for it.

LOUISE: Yes I know you're right. We'll go and watch it with the others. (*Takes* DAVID*'s sleeve.*) He needs some more suitable clothes now. Throw these revolting things away. (*She takes the stage spectacles which* DAVID*'s been holding and throws them upstage.*) We'll see he returns to wherever he came from. He looks younger every minute – (*Surprised.*) he's quite a child really. Come on Nigel (*glancing at* KRAMER.) quick, he's got business to do.

NIGEL (*to* KRAMER, *beams*): I congratulate you – I think we've done it!

LOUISE (*holding* NIGEL's *arm*): You realise he'll ring you about everything now. (*They begin to go, looking at* CAROLINE.) Look that weird girl's still there, wonder what she wanted.

DAVID (*going with* LOUISE, *to* KRAMER): You did well up there, for a first time. I think you may well become a star.

LOUISE (*laughing as they go*): Nothing can go wrong now thank goodness, unless I twist my ankle on the way down which is possible . . .

JOHN (*smiles at* KRAMER): You seem to have done all right.

KRAMER (*to* JOHN *looking at* CAROLINE): I've just got some business to see to . . .

JOHN: I wouldn't mind having a talk with you sometime.

KRAMER (*sharp*): Yes. Next time you're in the area.

JOHN (*slight self-mocking smile*): I want your autograph.

KRAMER (*sharp*): I don't think so.

JOHN (*genuine*): You think I'm joking. I'm going for a walk, I can't sleep yet. Somewhere out there's the sea – (*He smiles.*) maybe I should just swim out for several miles. I'll look out for your picture in the papers. (*He glances at* CAROLINE, *slight smile.*) So she's going to have time with you. (*He moves to go.*) I'll put you on the front of my new album, that's an idea. Don't worry it will be listenable to. I still manage to smuggle in some content underneath the pap. I'll have a track written about you.

KRAMER (*sharp*): Thanks.

JOHN (*slight smile*): You think I'm joking, which is sad.

He stares at the untouched table and the melting food then he goes. CAROLINE *and* KRAMER *alone on stage.* KRAMER *glances around for a second he lifts something off the crammed table.*

KRAMER: What a waste! (*He looks at her.*) Now for you Miss Murray.

CAROLINE (*looking up*): Now for me. (*Glances around.*) Shouldn't there be witnesses?

KRAMER: No we don't need witnesses. (*He looks at her.*) Though you were found with drugs on you.

CAROLINE: But I wasn't!

KRAMER: – and you assaulted a police officer, if you apologise to me I'm going to let you go free.

Pause.

CAROLINE (*tensing*): Apologise for what?

KRAMER: For what you did.

CAROLINE: But you know quite well I didn't do anything.

KRAMER (*standing the other side of the stage*): Just apologise to me for what you did. Come and stand here and say you're sorry and I'll let you go.

Silence. CAROLINE *is sitting on the ground holding an empty wine glass.*

CAROLINE: NO. I will not do that.

KRAMER (*quiet*): What do you mean!

CAROLINE: I mean I won't apologise to you – because I've done nothing wrong. And you know I haven't. (*Stares at him.*) I'm not going to crawl to you like all the others.

KRAMER: I don't know what you mean by that remark.

CAROLINE: I want a witness here.

KRAMER (*sharp*): I told you you don't need witnesses.

CAROLINE: It's funny them pouring out their hearts to you, for you have total contempt for all of them haven't you. For everyone really. (KRAMER *remains completely still.*) I mean you even spoke about your own daughter as if she hardly existed – just an object in your house which you watched.

KRAMER *does not react.*

I don't think you even like Stephen very much do you?

No reaction.

I doubt if you even feel lonely.

KRAMER: I will repeat once more – either you apologise to me or I will have you arrested.

He stares at her. CAROLINE *shakes her head.*

I don't think you understand, do you. (*He stares at her for a moment, his voice unnaturally quiet.*) A boy was killed in a motor-bike accident this week. I went and told the mother in person. By myself.

She was a pale very ordinary woman, standing there in the kitchen – but she trusted me totally. And after I spoke to her, she said 'I'm unhappy and yet in a way I don't feel anything'. She didn't even weep. I was there one hour and she didn't even cry. She didn't cry for him all that day or the next. It was like an anaesthetic. She hardly noticed the pain. For I have this power . . . to make people feel less. I have seen violent things my whole life, things you cannot imagine and now they have no effect on me at all. (*He is standing very still.*) I meet people all the time as I work – I *know* what they want.

CAROLINE: I don't believe that for a moment.

KRAMER: You cannot argue with me I'm afraid. (*He stands very still, staring at her.*) People talk to me on a first meeting more than they have done to their neighbours in a whole lifetime. The youngsters too, running towards me now (*He stares at her.*) like her.

I drive round the city at night, watching people sometimes, totally by myself; they can't see me but I can see them. I see them as they really are. They want a few certainties again, to feel safe, to have their women back in their house where they belong. (*Slight smile.*) To be told things won't change any more, to be able to believe there's a God in heaven again. To be protected.

(*He stares at her.*) And I found it doesn't matter exactly what you say or even if one doesn't believe every word oneself. It doesn't have to be real. It's the way it's done . . . the right tone of voice. They all want to be reassured now – like this lot here tonight. Gently soothed. (*His voice rising louder.*) And I have a talent for that you see . . . a power. A way of handling people. I've worked at it every day of every year . . . as gradually I've been able to use it more and more. (*Louder:*) And now it cannot be contradicted. (*Slight pause.*) Because people trust me. They

believe me.

CAROLINE (*staring at him*): But I don't. I don't believe in you at all.

KRAMER: (*staring back, loud*): I told you – I cannot be argued with.

CAROLINE: You don't believe in anything really do you – except your own ambition.

He just stares straight at her.

I won't do what you want.

KRAMER: (*surprised, his voice hard*): You won't? You stupid child – you realise evening classes won't be much good to you if you have a criminal record.

CAROLINE: I'll find a way – (*Her voice firm.*) I don't respond to threats I'm afraid.

KRAMER (*suddenly loud*): Apologise to me now!

Silence. No reaction from CAROLINE.

He explodes, his voice full of fury. DID YOU HEAR ME? COME HERE.

She doesn't move.

COME OVER HERE . . . (*Really loud:*) COME HERE!

Silence.

CAROLINE: No. (*Her voice is calm and firm.*)

STEPHEN *enters and stands up-stage.*

KRAMER (*stares at* CAROLINE, *very quiet*): I was going to let you go. (*He glances at* STEPHEN.) We are going to prosecute. Take her in and charge her with assaulting a police officer and carrying illegal drugs. (*He stares at* CAROLINE.) We'll let the courts decide if there's a case to answer, and I expect they will.

STEPHEN *moves up to her.*

CAROLINE: Can . . . can I talk to someone. I mean ring . . .

KRAMER: (*cutting in*): No you will be taken straight down into custody.

CAROLINE: Oh Christ. (*Her head goes down for a moment; she begins to cry, then looks up, suddenly smiles at him, sharp, confident.*) At least you see *I* can still cry.

STEPHEN *moves her towards the exit.*

KRAMER (*without emotion as she is moving to the exit*): It's a pity, I enjoyed meeting you.

Music has begun in the distance. It is bright morning light, the arc light is still on.

STEPHEN (*at the exit*): You want anything?

KRAMER: No thank you.

STEPHEN: Going home sir?

KRAMER: No I don't think so. I think . . . I'll have a slight sleep in the car.

STEPHEN *and* CAROLINE *go.*

KRAMER (*very quiet into the walkie-talkie*): Music a little louder . . . I like this piece.

'Oh For the Wings of a Dove', DAVID's *stage piece, plays louder but still distant. The arc lights click off in unison.* KRAMER *stares at them for a split second, standing in the middle of the stage. He stares at the long table of untouched food. Then he moves towards the car, stops and picks up a piece of litter on the way. He reaches the car, opens the door and climbs on to the back seat. He lies down full length on the seat, then leans forward and shuts the car door.*

Fade

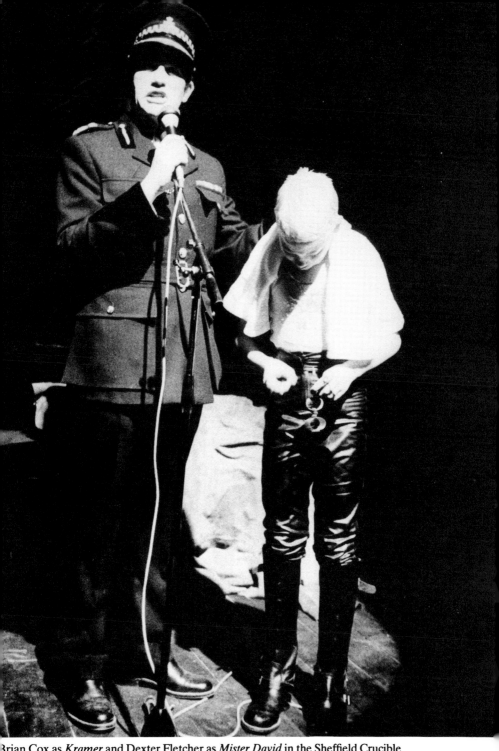

Brian Cox as *Kramer* and Dexter Fletcher as *Mister David* in the Sheffield Crucible production. Photo: Viewfinder Associates

Dexter Fletcher as *Mister David* in the Sheffield Crucible production.
Photo: Viewfinder Associates